# EIGHTH AIR FORCE
## STORY

## ...IN WORLD WAR II

**KENN C. RUST**

PUBLISHED BY

P.O. BOX 33
TEMPLE CITY, CALIF. 91780

Overseas distributor
W. E. Hersant, Ltd.
228 Archway Road,
Highgate
London, N. 6. England

# INTRODUCTION AND ACKNOWLEDGMENT

It was some twenty years ago that I began researching for a book on the Eighth Air Force, gathering photos and collecting reference material, some two thousand pages of it, from AAF sources. Fate, however, dictated that the history itself was not to be written until now, for this series. In preparing this history every effort has been made to provide a coordinated, overall picture, with incisive views of significant moments and events in the development and operations of the Eighth Air Force—the largest AAF Air Force in World War II in every sense of the word. All the important facets of the Eighth's activities, from birth to V-E Day, are treated and there is coverage for all of its combat units, including at least one photo of an aircraft of each of its fifty-five bomber and fighter groups.

Unlike the other books in this series, a Tactical Unit History chart has not been included as such in this book, but the relevant tactical record information has been coordinated with the markings drawings for each bomber and fighter group and the text for Other Units.

Seventeen tables have been included to give the closest possible look at key Eighth performances. Statistical numbers in these tables and the text are as accurate as possible, but it should be pointed out that when various official Eighth Air Force records are consulted for a given action there are occasions when differing numbers of aircraft lost, dispatched, attacking, etc. are found, so that in those cases exact figures may be forever in question. In presenting victory claims of enemy aircraft encountered in the air, the claims are given in three figures (12-3-4), the figures representing the number of aircraft claimed destroyed-probably destroyed-damaged. Victory claims against enemy aircraft attacked on the ground are given in two figures (12-3), the figures representing enemy aircraft claimed destroyed-damaged.

Over the years more individuals than I can recall have helped to make this book possible, and I would like to express my sincerest thanks to each of them here. More specifically I would like to thank Bill Hess for his assistance in checking over, verifying and finalizing the list of aces and for his other help; Roger A. Freeman for proofreading the main text for me and for his other assistance; Lt. Col. M. E. Bodington, Chief, and Capt. Peter R. Hefler of the Magazine and Book Branch Department of the Air Force for their aid in providing most necessary photographs; and to the staff of the Aerospace Studies Institute at Maxwell AFB, Alabama who helped me acquire material from the archives over the years.

Others I would also like to thank are: William T. Ashley, Thomas M. Barnett, Dana Bell, Ken Blakebrough, Allan G. Blue, Ray E. Bowers, Royal D. Frey, Garry L. Fry, Robert Louden, Harry Miller, John Preston, William T. Searby, William L. Swisher, Dwayne M. Tabatt, Osamu Tagaya, Ernest L. True, Phil Yant and Gerry J. Zwanenburg.

Kenn C. Rust

January, 1978

# COLOR CODE CHIPS

 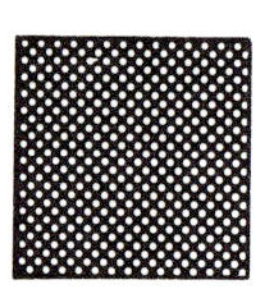  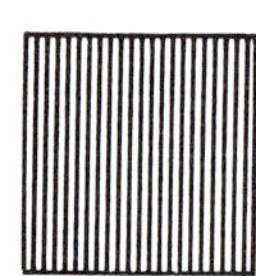   

| Red | Blue | Yellow | Green | Black | Olive Drab | Lt. Grey |



Typography
**TRADE TYPE**
San Gabriel, California 91776

# EIGHTH AIR FORCE ...IN WORLD WAR II

## TABLE OF CONTENTS



## ABBREVIATIONS USED IN THIS BOOK

| | |
|---|---|
| AA — Antiaircraft | H.E. — High Explosive |
| AAF — Army Air Force | IB — Incendiary Bomb |
| A/D — Air Depot | IP — Initial Point |
| A/F — Airfield | I/T — Industrial Transportation Target |
| ASR — Air Sea Rescue | KIA — Killed In Action |
| ATT — Attacking | MIA — Missing in Action |
| BG — Bomb Group | MPI — Mean Point of Impact |
| BS — Bomb Squadron | M/Y — Marshalling Yard |
| CBO — Combined Bomber Offensive | NMF — Natural Metal Finish |
| CBW — Combat Bomb Wing | OD — Olive Drab |
| CCRC — Combat Crew Replacement Center | P/A — Port Area |
| C.O. — Commanding Officer | PFF — Pathfinder Force |
| CW — Combat Wing | POW — Prisoner of War |
| DIS — Dispatched | PRI — Primary |
| E/A — Enemy Aircraft | RAF — Royal Air Force |
| ETO — European Theater of Operations | S/Y — Shipyard |
| FG — Fighter Group | T/O — Target of Opportunity |
| FS — Fighter Squadron | U/B — U-boat Base |
| GAF — German Air Force | U.K. — United Kingdom |
| GP — General Purpose | |

## COVER PHOTO FROM USAF

*Boeing B-17G Fortresses of the
381st Bomb Group in the latter
months of World War II.*

PROFILE DRAWINGS BY PAUL R. MATT

# EIGHTH AIR FORCE HISTORY

Following United States entry into World War II, American President Franklin Roosevelt and British Prime Minister Winston Churchill met in a series of conversations known as the Arcadia Conference in Washington, D.C., from 23 December 1941 to 14 January 1942. Their purpose was to establish priorities and define, with their chiefs of staff, how the war was to be conducted.

From the Arcadia Conference a number of key decisions emerged. The main Allied war effort would be made against Germany first while containing the Japanese in the Pacific. An American air force would be moved to the United Kingdom as soon as possible. And a joint occupation of French North Africa and French Northwest Africa was of prime strategic importance for the complete encirclement of Germany and the safeguarding of Allied sea communications.

Plans for the latter were drawn up under the code name SUPER GYMNAST (laster referred to as GYMNAST), and a U.S. "Fifth Air Force" was designated to furnish air support. But the initial designation was soon changed to Eighth Air Force, and on 28 January 1942 the Eighth Air Force was activated at Savannah, Georgia for SUPER GYMNAST.

Less than five weeks after activation, however, on 3 March 1942, the newborn Eighth found itself without a mission when SUPER GYMNAST was relegated to the status of an academic study. Meanwhile, though, plans had been underway to establish an American Air Force in Britain (AAFIB). When they were fully germinated the "unattached" Eighth was named, 8 April 1942, to serve as the air force to be rushed to England.

Immediately, the Eighth began to receive combat units with which to fulfill its new task. The first ones were the freshly activated 92nd, 97th and 301st Bomb Groups (Heavy), all with B-17E Flying Fortresses, the 15th Bomb Squadron (Light) with A-20s, and the 1st and 31st Pursuit (soon Fighter) Groups with P-38s and P-39s respectively.

No sooner were the new units assigned than the War Department directed the Eighth, on 27 April 1942, to prepare the 97th, 1st and 31st Groups for overseas movement by the 1st of June. The Eighth was on its way to England, where its mission would be to initiate a daylight air offensive against the battle-wise Germans, even though its tactics were unproven and its units scarcely fledged.

Preparations for the movement of the air echelons of the first units to England proceeded smoothly and everything was in hand when, on 1 June 1942, an interruption occurred. The movement was suddenly suspended. A great Japanese fleet was sailing on Midway and the remainder of the U.S. fleet in the Pacific. If the Japanese won the forthcoming Battle of Midway, Hawaii and the West Coast would be wide open to attack. Such an eventuality had to be countered, and on 2 June (as aircraft on the West Coast were rushed to Hawaii) the 97th Bomb Group was ordered to the West Coast. As soon as it was in place the 1st Fighter Group headed west also.

The P-38s of the 1st Fighter Group were barely on their way, however, when the Battle of Midway came to an end, a great victory for the United States. The emergency ended as quickly as it had begun. On 6 June the 1st was ordered back to Maine, and five days later the 97th also headed back to New England. On 12 June, the 31st Fighter Group air echelon, less its P-39 aircraft, departed for England by sea. Six days later, the 1st and 97th Groups, plus the C-47 equipped 60th Troop Carrier Group, began flying their planes to England.

The first leg took the planes to Presque Isle, Maine. There they were organized into flights, one B-17 to four P-38s, with the additional B-17s and the C-47s to proceed as separate elements. The first elements, totalling eighteen B-17s, departed Presque Isle on 23 June. They were followed by the first B-17/P-38 flights, headed for Goose Bay, Labrador. From there it was on to Greenland, but even with summer's arrival the forbidding North Atlantic was no playground. On 15 July two flights ran into heavy weather, and six P-38s and two B-17/P-38 flights, headed for Goose Bay, Labrador. From later the last element of the first movement, two B-17s leading eight P-38s, departed Presque Isle. On 27 July all ten landed safely at Prestwick, Scotland. Although aircraft had been lost, no serious injuries were suffered during the entire operation.

While the first groups were arriving, men of the 15th Bomb Squadron (which had come to England by sea in May) became the first U.S. crews to go into action over Europe. The Squadron's crews had been training on Bostons with 226 Squadron of the RAF. On 29 June one 15th crew flew a Boston on a twelve plane raid by 226 Squadron against the marshalling yard at Hazebrouck, France. But the big day was the Fourth of July, when six U.S. crews joined six RAF crews to take a dozen RAF Bostons on a low level mission against four German airfields in Holland.

The twelve Bostons departed England on schedule and went right down on the deck crossing the English Channel. About ten miles off the Dutch coast they came upon several fishing boats. One of these sent an early warning to the German Command in the Low Countries of the approach of British light bombers. A few minutes later the Bostons came in over the dike land and headed for their objectives.

One three plane flight, including two AAF crews, failed to find its target and returned without bombing. Another, including one AAF crew, successfully bombed the airfield at Haamstede without loss. The third flight, including one AAF crew, attacked Bergen/Alkamaar and met strong antiaircraft fire as they raced in on the deck. The flight's U.S. crew was shot down just after bombing and an RAF crew was also lost.

The other two U.S. crews were in the three plane flight which attacked De Kooy airfield.

At De Kooy, Capt. Charles C. Kegelman (who'd piloted the Boston of the lone AAF crew on the 29 June mission) was flying the number two position in the British led flight with another AAF crew in the number three position. The flight passed through the light flak of De Kooy's outer defenses, three miles from the target, without damage, made a flat turn over an open area before reaching the inner defenses and headed for the target.

Seconds later the flight came in on De Kooy and the inner ring of light flak opened up. To Capt. Kegelman and his crew it seemed as though the Germans were aiming only at them. Tracers were everywhere about their plane. Then a staccato tattoo suddenly rattled through it, and the right propeller flew off and the engine was set afire. At almost the same instant, while Capt. Kegelman fought to control his aircraft, the bomb load was released and arced down onto the airfield. The lightened plane bounded into the air and then settled quickly even as Kegelman applied full power to the one remaining engine. The tail hit the ground, the whole machine shuddered as a section of the lower rear fuselage was ripped out, but somehow Kegelman managed to pull the plane free of the ground and get her back into the air. Still the struggling Boston was surrounded by enemy fire, a good part of it coming from a flak tower just outside the airfield. Kegelman kicked his plane around and headed for the flak tower, blazing away with his forward firing machine guns. Before he was half way to the tower it stopped shooting back.

After that Capt. Kegelman managed to get his Boston out of the area and fly it back to its base at Swanton Morley, using all his skill to bring plane and crew home. The other U.S. crew attacking De Kooy had not made it; they were shot down in flames near the target.

U.S. airmen of the 15th Squadron, though they still had a great deal to learn, had proven their worth and that whatever job there was to do American airmen could do it.

After an operation on 12 July, the 15th Squadron began converting to AAF Boston III's and A-20B's.

By August, additional Eighth units were on their way to England. The 301st Bomb Group's new B-17F's began arriving in England on 9 August; the equally new B-17F's of the 92nd Bomb Group began flying across the North Atlantic in squadron formation on 15 August with the last squadron flying over on 26-27 August, all making it without loss; the 14th Fighter Group brought its P-38s safely across and began arriving at Atcham on 18 August; while the 64th Troop Carrier Group came over with its C-47s, and the 52nd Fighter Group crossed the Atlantic by sea without its P-39s.

Meanwhile, the basic doctrine of Eighth Air Force operations was put forth in a directive issued by Gen. George Marshall. Eighth bombing missions were to be provided with fighter support by the RAF, either directly or by synchronizing missions with RAF fighter sweeps. The role of U.S. fighter units would be to provide close support for bomber operations, and they were not to be used for the defense of the United Kingdom or integrated into RAF Fighter Command.

Strategic control of operations was vested in the British government by agreement and was to include the development of general strategic directives outlining the immediate purposes and broad objectives. Designation of targets and tactical control of operations was to be worked out jointly by the commander of the Eighth and the British Air Ministry's Assistant Chief of Air Staff (Operations). The overall objective of operations would be to gain air supremacy over Western Europe so as to support a combined land, sea and air movement across the Channel when the time came.

In essence then, the evolvement of an independent Eighth Air Force would be based on the more than three years of operational experience of the Royal Air Force. That experience was an extremely valuable heritage, and into it the Eighth intended to infuse the American principles of "pinpoint strategic bombardment" and its corollary "daylight operations". Of the latter principle, however, the British were openly dubious.

One British spokesman warned that the B-17s, and the B-24D Liberators which were soon to join them, must not be thrown into a daylight offensive so "that the flower of America's regular Army Air Force is not squandered on a type of operation that experience would judge unwise." It was also felt that U.S. heavy bombers, "fine flying machines" though they were, should not join the night offensive either, since they carried small bomb loads and were considered slow. Instead, there was a plea that the Eighth's B-17s and B-24s should be turned over to Coastal Command and that American crews join with RAF crews on Lancasters and Halifaxes to further the bombardment attack on Germany by *night*. In other words, the Eighth should forgo daylight operations and use its crews by night to supplement the efforts of Bomber Command.

Despite such entreaties and warnings, however, the Eighth persevered with its intention to try out daylight techniques. Its leaders believed that the B-17E's and F's, armed with ten strategically placed .50 caliber machine guns and able to operate efficiently at high altitudes (20,000 feet and above), would be able to defend themselves from enemy fighter attack and fly high enough to be outside the effective range of much of the German antiaircraft defenses.

The Eighth's confidence and determination were affirmed by an August 1942 Joint Directive which stated that the first phase of Eighth Air Force operations would see "American day bomber forces under British fighter protection reinforced by American fighter forces . . . attack suitable objectives within the radius of British fighter cover." The Eighth would try precision daylight bombing attacks, but it would safeguard its efforts by taking the opportunity to operate under the fullest RAF fighter protection available.

Throughout the Eighth's command structure, everyone was anxious to prove it could successfully carry out daylight bomber operations. At the apex of that pyramid structure was 8th Air Force Headquarters at Bushy Park (code name WIDEWING) under Maj. Gen. Carl Spaatz, who would be succeeded by Maj. Gen. Ira C. Eaker on 1 December 1942 and Lt. Gen. James H. Doolittle on 6 January 1944. Under 8th AF HQ were the four basic commands of the air force —VIII Ground Air Support Command at Membury (designed to provide for the training and operations of air forces in direct support of an invasion of Europe, so that it did not have an immediate role to play), VIII Service Command at Bushy Park, VIII Fighter Command at Bushey Hall (code name AJAX), and VIII Bomber Command at High Wycombe (code name PINETREE).

Under the latter, to give closer control of groups, was the first of the Eighth's wing organizations — the 1st Bomb Wing which became fully activated on 19 August 1942 at Brampton Grange and took control of the 92nd, 97th and 301st Bomb Groups. Another such unit, the 2nd Bomb Wing, would arrive from the U.S. in September and take up station at Old Catton. It would control B-24 groups.

While the bombers were readying for combat, the fighter units had been learning the ropes under RAF Fighter Command tutelage. Leading the way was the 31st Fighter Group which, after arriving in June, had reequipped with Spitfire V's. On 26 July 1942, six of its pilots became the first AAF fighter pilots to fly operationally in the ETO. The six included the three squadron C.O.'s and Lt. Col. Albert P. Clark, the Group Executive Officer. They joined with an RAF Spitfire Squadron from Biggin Hill on a fighter sweep against objectives in France between Gravelines, St. Omer and Abbeville. During a brief scuffle with the Luftwaffe, Lt. Col. Clark was shot down. He became a POW and spent the remainder of the war at Stalag-Luft III. The other pilots on the mission returned without claims or loss.

The 31st Fighter Group itself went operational on 5 August, sending out eleven of its Spitfires on a practice Rodeo (a fighter sweep over enemy territory without bombers). Four days later two Spitfires were scrambled on a defensive patrol in which they managed to damage a German recon plane — the first claim for VIII Fighter Command.

On 17 August 1942, the awaited day came and the Eighth carried out its first bomber mission — a daylight, precision, high level attack on the Sotteville marshalling yards at Rouen in France by twelve B-17E's of the 97th Bomb Group. An hour and a quarter before the mission six other 97th B-17E's flew a diversion for the main mission. Three failed to meet their escort of 62 RAF Spit V's and aborted. The other three flew the diversion to Dunkirk with an escort of 121 Spit V's, 12 of which were from the 31st FG. No German fighters were encountered.

At 1627 the main force began taking off and formed into two six plane elements, the first led by Col. Frank Armstrong, C.O. of the 97th, and the second led by "Yankee Doodle" with the Commander of VIII Bomber Command, Gen. Ira Eaker, aborad. Escorted by 48 RAF Spit IX's, the Flying Fortresses crossed into France near St. Valery and spotted their target ten minutes before release time. Without meeting any fighter opposition the twelve planes bombed separately in formation from 23,000 feet while flying through moderate but accurate flak. From 1739 to 1746, 18 tons of bombs were dropped. The small number of German fighters, mainly FW 190s, which then arrived were handled by the RAF escort. It claimed 2-4-5 for the loss of three Spitfires. Only two enemy fighters got near the bombers, and one was claimed as damaged by a ball turret gunner.

As for the bombing, it was poor and widespread but knocked out a few lines and destroyed some cars and facilities. One bomb landed within 1000 feet of the MPI and 17 within 2000 feet. No lasting damage was done to the yard.

When all planes had returned to base it was found that one had sustained hits in four places from a flak burst, and another had been hit once by an enemy fighter. Rouen had been a modest and not very effective beginning from which no definite conclusions could be drawn. More missions would be needed to prove the case for daylight precision bombing.

Two days later the Eighth took part in the Combined Landing Operations at Dieppe. These were planned by the British with two purposes in mind. To try out large scale landing techniques as they would be employed when the Allies initiated a full invasion to return to the German-held Continent of Europe. And to bring a large portion of the Luftwaffe's carefully husbanded force of 470 aircraft in the West to battle so that force could be seriously damaged.

The plan called for 6,000 Canadian and British troops plus 50 U.S. Rangers to land at Dieppe and hold their bridgehead for a few hours before retiring. In the air RAF and Eighth Air Force planes would support the landing, the fighters engaging the Luftwaffe at every opportunity.

The landings began at 0300 hours on 19 August 1942, and the troops remained for nine hours before withdrawing to England, suffering 3,650 casualties. RAF Bostons and Blenheims laid smoke for the troops and attacked gun positions. The B-17s of the 97th Bomb Group, escorted by 48 RAF fighters, made their first substantial contribution to the war effort, bombing the Luftwaffe fighter base at Abbeville/Drucat and putting it out of action for two vital hours.

Of 24 B-17E's dispatched, 22 dropped 108 600-lb H.E. bombs and 41 250-lbs incendiary bombs on Abbeville/Drucat at 1030 while encountering moderate to intense heavy flak. Twenty-seven bombs landed in the NW dispersal area, three close to aircraft hangars, one a direct hit destroying a hangar and three near a light flak position. Several enemy fighters were seen but no claims were made. All B-17s returned safely, three damaged slightly by flak splinters.

By day's end, the RAF had flown 2,339 fighter sorties and the Eighth (31st Group) had flown 123. Losses were 106 RAF aircraft and 8 Spitfires of the 31st, whose pilots claimed 1-3-3, the first enemy plane to be shot down in Europe by an AAF pilot being an FW 190 claimed by Lt. Samuel S. Junkin,

| EARLY EIGHTH OPERATIONS--1942 | | | | | |
|---|---|---|---|---|---|
| DATE | TARGET | DIS | ATT | TONS | LOST | CLAIMS* |
| 17 Aug | Rouen M/Y | 12 | 12 | 18 | 0 | 0-0-1 |
| | Diversion | 6 | | | 0 | 0-0-0 |
| 19 Aug | Abbeville A/F | 24 | 22 | 37 | 0 | 0-0-0 |
| 20 Aug | Amiens M/Y | 12 | 11 | 23 | 0 | 0-0-0 |
| 21 Aug | Rotterdam S/Y | 12 | Recalled | | 0 | 2-5-6 |
| 24 Aug | Le Trait S/Y | 12 | 12 | 24 | 0 | 0-0-0 |
| 27 Aug | Rotterdam S/Y | 9 | 7 | 13 | 0 | 0-0-0 |
| 28 Aug | Meaulte A/D | 14 | 11 | 25 | 0 | 0-0-0 |
| 29 Aug | Courtrai A/F | 13 | 12 | 28 | 0 | 0-1-2 |
| 5 Sep | Rouen M/Y | 37 | 31 | 72 | 0 | 0-0-0 |
| 6 Sep | Meaulte A/D | 41 | 30 | 67 | 2 | 4-19-20 |
| | St. Omer A/F's | 13 | 13 | 26 | 0 | 0-0-0 |
| 7 Sep | Rotterdam S/Y | 29 | 7 | 18 | 0 | 12-10-12 |
| | Utrecht T/O | | 2 | 5 | 0 | 0-0-0 |
| 26 Sep | Cherbourg A/F | 27 | Recalled | | 0 | 0-0-0 |
| | Morlaix A/F | 19 | Aborted | | 0 | 0-0-0 |
| | Diversion | 17 | | | 0 | 0-0-0 |
| 2 Oct | Meaulte A/D | 43 | 34 | 69 | 0 | 4-5-1 |
| | St. Omer A/F | 6 | 6 | 13 | 0 | 5-4-4 |
| | Diversion | 13 | | | 0 | 0-0-0 |
| 9 Oct | Lille I/T | 108 | 69 | 157 | 4 | 25-38-44 |
| | St. Omer A/F | | 6 | 12 | 0 | 0-0-0 |
| | Courtrai A/F | | 2 | 5 | 0 | 0-0-0 |
| | Roubaix T/O | | 2 | 3 | 0 | 0-0-0 |
| | Diversion | 7 | | | 0 | 0-0-0 |
| 21 Oct | Lorient U/B | 90 | 15 | 30 | 3 | 10-4-3 |
| | Cherbourg A/F | 17 | 9 | 8 | 0 | 0-0-0 |
| 7 Nov | Brest U/B | 68 | 34 | 79 | 0 | 4-3-7 |
| | Diversion | 7 | | | 0 | 0-0-0 |
| 8 Nov | Lille I/T | 38 | 30 | 73 | 1 | 10-4-13 |
| | Abbeville A/F | 15 | 11 | 28 | 0 | 1-2-1 |
| 9 Nov | St. Nazaire U/B | 47 | 43 | 114 | 3 | 0-0-0 |
| 14 Nov | St. Nazaire U/B | 34 | 24 | 57 | 0 | 0-0-0 |
| | Diversion | 6 | | | 0 | 0-0-0 |
| * Some early Claims were later scaled down. | | | | | |

Spitfire Vb of the 4th Fighter Group, 336th Fighter Squadron. Pilot was Capt. Leroy Gover. (Lee Gover)

who was himself shot down but rescued from the Channel. The landings had achieved most objectives, and the air fighting had cost the Luftwaffe 48 planes.

During the last twelve days of August, the 97th flew six more bombing missions in shallow penetrations of France and Holland. The bombing was fair to poor, and on 21 August there was no bombing at all as the nine B-17s which reached the Dutch Coast were recalled when their fighter escort had to withdraw. The recall came a few moments too late, however. Just as the nine turned back they were jumped by twenty Me 109s and FW 190s. A running fight ensued, and the pilot and copilot of one B-17 were wounded, the latter dying soon afterward, but the damaged Fortress made it back to England. The tail gunner of this aircraft had downed an FW 190, and claims for all crews in the 20 minute battle were 2-5-6.

For the first time the Flying Fortresses had met enemy fighters in a head to head confrontation, and they had proved they could defend themselves in aerial combat. The prognosticators of doom, who'd said bombers could not survive fighter attacks in daylight, had been proved wrong.

On 28 August, the 97th attacked the modern Avion Potez aircraft factory at Meaulte, which the Germans were using as a repair depot for their fighters based in northern France. Eleven B-17s dropped 72 500-lb and 12 1100-lb bombs from 22,500 to 24,000 feet, while their escort beat off an attempted interception by a dozen FW 109s.

The first four bombs burst almost two miles from the target, 29 to 36 bombs burst over a mile away, 10 to 12 hit half a mile away, 15 to 19 bombs burst near the depot, and a series of large bursts stradled the town of Meaulte. Of all bombs dropped, one had destroyed a hangar. The bombing had been without question very poor. The Eighth's bombers still had to prove they could bomb accurately in combat.

Also in the last dozen days of August, Eighth fighter operations continued, 199 sorties being flown without claims or losses, and two new groups went operational. On 24 August, Spitfires of the 2nd and 4th Squadrons of the 52nd Fighter Group carried out the Group's first mission when six were scrambled to intercept reported enemy raiders. Five days later, the 1st Group went into action, twice scrambling two P-38s to intercept enemy raiders.

On 29 September, the three RAF Eagle Squadrons, pilots (American volunteers serving in the RAF) and planes, were transferred to the AAF. They were incorporated into the 4th Fighter Group, which had been activated in England to receive them on 12 September. The ex-Eagles of the 4th would fly their first mission with the Eighth on 2 October when 23 Spit V's made a sweep of the French coast.

Only four bombing missions (half the August number) were dispatched by the Eighth Air Force in September. The first, on 5 September, revisited the Sotteville marshalling yards at Rouen and marked the first time a mission was carried out by two groups. Twelve B-17F's of the 301st Group, on its initial mission, and 25 from the 97th were dispatched, and 31 dropped 198 H.E. bombs on the target. Twenty-two bombs fell within 1000 feet of the MPI and 34 within 2000 feet.

Next day, the Eighth dispatched its first three group mission, as the 92nd Bomb Group joined operations. In all 54 heavies were sent against two targets—while a dozen 15th BS Bostons carried out a diversion, attacking the Abbeville/Drucat airfield. The main target was the depot at Meaulte which had been so badly missed nine days before. This time the bombing at Meaulte was only fair; a ten-bay hangar received a direct hit and shops were damaged, but the facility was in no way put out of action.

However, the real story of the mission was the air battle precipitated with some forty enemy fighters, mainly FW 190s. Near Meaulte the Eighth lost its first bomber, as a B-17F of the 97th Group was shot down with four crewmen being seen to bail out as the plane went down. A second plane, a B-17E

A Spitfire Vb of the 31st Fighter Group, 309th Fighter Squadron which was left behind in England by the Group when it went to North Africa. Photo taken 15 March 1943. (USAF)

of the 92nd, was so badly hit by enemy fighters that it went down in the Channel on return, and no trace of its crew was found. Another 92nd B-17E was badly damaged, the tail gunner killed and two other members of the crew fatally wounded, but it made it back to England. The returned crews claimed 4-19-20 enemy fighters, but in the heat of battle they had (as would so often happen in the history of the Eighth) over-counted. Actually, they had downed only a few enemy fighters while damaging several more.

Blooded now, the Eighth went to Rotterdam the very next day, the 7th. Enemy fighter opposition, steadily beginning to draw a bead on the Fortresses, was nearly continuous from the Dutch coast despite fighter escort and heavy clouds. The latter interferred with bombing, and only seven Forts dropped their loads on the Wilton Ship Yard, scoring one hit in the target area. In the air battle crews claimed 12-10-12, while two Fortresses were shot up and sustained casualties.

Elusive Meaulte was attacked for the third time on 2 October, and this time the Eighth further proved it was coming of age and that in time its daylight strategic bombing would be as effective as it had contended.

While 13 92nd B-17s flew a diversion and 6 of the 97th bombed the German fighter base at St. Omer/Longuenesse (encountering some thirty enemy fighters of which they claimed 5-4-4 without loss), 18 Forts from the 97th and 25 from the 301st set out for Meaulte. There was no flak as 34 B-17s dropped 240 500-lb H.E. bombs and 70 250-lb incendiaries from 22,000 to 27,000 feet. The depot took 5 to 6 direct hits from the 301st and 5 to 10 from the 97th. The main assembly hangar and the prototype shop were knocked out, and the depot was put out of action for a period of time. The bombers had fifty encounters with enemy fighters, which concentrated on the 301st. The 97th claimed 1-0-0 while the 301st claimed 3-5-1 and had six B-17s damaged, one crash landing at Gatwick with three crew members wounded.

Battle casualties in killed, missing and wounded continued and increased as operations progressed, but they were not the only losses suffered. There were also non-combat casualties which took a steady toll of Eighth manpower. One such case resulted from an incident on 2 October.

The 306th Bomb Group, soon to go into action, was flying a practice mission over England that day. At 26,000 feet the waist gunner of one Fortress passed out because of anoxia. The pilot put the plane into a vertical dive for lower altitude, but when he tried to pull out at 20,000 feet the cables snapped, the right wing and engines pulled off and a bomb bay door ripped loose and sheared off the tail section. The Tail Gunner was trapped in his position, hurtling down end over end. He tried to smash his way out through the glass and failed, then kicked his way through the skin of the plane and began to wriggle out until his shoulders became wedged. Struggling frantically, he was blown clear at about one thousand feet and just had time to get his parachute open before hitting the ground physically unharmed.

The plane crashed about 100 yards from where he landed in the middle of a British antiaircraft battery. The Tail Gunner and several British soldiers ran over to the burning fuselage and tried to pull one of the men out through the waist window, but it quickly became apparent he was crushed and dead. The next morning, after a night of the cold shakes, the Tail Gunner went out to the wreck with his Commanding Officer. There he saw the charred bodies of the other eight men who had been in the plane. In the following days he had recurring dreams of plane crashes, had to force himself to enter a plane and was startled by whistling and whining noises which reminded him of the wind shrieking through the jagged tail section as it fell from the wreck.

In spite of this, he went on operations and flew five combat missions. On one, serving as waist gunner, his plane was hit by flak. The blast blew pieces of canvas over his head and into his mouth and wrapped some control wires around his neck. He was so frightened when he freed himself that he almost bailed out without orders. On a later mission, an FW 190 appeared fifty feet behind the tail turret, and he saw his tracer bullets enter where the oxygen bottles are located. There was a flash of flame and the German spun down out of control. After the incident he felt in a way that he had been responsible for causing another man to go through an experience such as he had suffered.

The 26 year old Tail Gunner was subsequently taken off operations by his medical officer, although he was afraid he would be thought of as a "quitter" and as "yellow". Nothing was farther from the truth — he'd given all he had, taken all he could. He was one of many men, equally heroes, lost in the fight without actually falling to the enemy.

The growing power of the Eighth was fully demonstrated on 9 October when the 306th Bomb Group with B-17s and the 93rd Bomb Group, first of the Eighth's B-24D Liberator groups, flew their first mission. Their debut enabled the Eighth to send out five bomb groups and dispatch over one hundred bombers for the first time. A total of 108 (24 of them B-24s) took off to attack two targets in the city of Lille — the steel and engineering works of the Cie. de Fives-Lille, and the Ateliers d'Hellemmes locomotive, carriage and wagon works — while 7 B-17s of the 92nd flew a diversion. The bombers heading for Lille were escorted by 61 Spit IX's, 36 1st FG P-38s, 23 Spit VI's and 36 Spit V's.

At Lille 10 B-24s and 59 B-17s bombed their primary targets between 0930 and 0948 — 10 others bombed targets of opportunity. In all 592 500-lb bombs were dropped on the two targets at Lille with ten hits recorded within 2000 feet of the MPI at Ateliers d'Hellemmes and twelve hits within 2000 feet of the MPI at Fives-Lille. There was no record of the 70 250-lb incendiaries dropped at Lille.

During a thirty minute period as the heavies came off the target at Lille, about fifty FW 190s and Me 109s made seventy passes at them. A B-17 of the 306th was shot down five miles south of Lille with eight crewmen bailing out. A B-24 of the 93rd was also shot down over France, and two B-17s went down in the Channel, one from the 92nd and one from the 301st. The latter's crew was picked up by the Air Sea Rescue service. Forty of the returning bombers were damaged, but the gunners felt they had very much held their own, claiming 25-38-44. However, that totalled more fighters than the Germans had in the air, and later claims were scaled down to 21-21-15. But even these were far too high.

Throughout the war, overly high claims by Eighth bombers (and also fighters) would be made. In the heat of battle, more than one gunner would often claim the same enemy fighter shot down; a gunner would believe he scored more telling hits than he did; and, despite increasing efforts, intelligence sections did not employ harsh enough methods (though they improved them) in assessing each gunner's claims.

Of the 25 enemy fighters first claimed shot down on the

**Boeing B-17E Flying Fortresses operated in 1942 by the 97th and 92nd Bomb Groups. (Myke Jacobs)**

Lille mission, a study of each claim by the author indicates that no more than eight fighters were destroyed (in five cases pilots were seen to bail out, a 109 and 190 were seen to disintegrate and a 109 was seen to crash). Four of the claims were probably duplications, five were made without adequate foundation, and eight enemy fighters claimed destroyed were in effect probably damaged. Yet even this appraisal does not concur with German records which show only two fighters lost to the bombers. There is, however, reason to believe German records did not show all their losses.

Whatever the true figures were for German fighter losses on 9 October, one fact remained. The bombers had proved they could defend themselves from concentrated enemy fighter attacks without exhorbitant losses. And though their claims were too high, the morale effect of such high claims offset increasing losses. Lille, therefore, and some preceding missions, guaranteed the reputation of the Eighth's heavies to do their job in spite of the Luftwaffe (though they still relied on escort) and assured the Eighth the chance to carry on its campaign of daylight, precision, strategic bombing.

But it wouldn't be easy. The defensive formations and armament of the heavies would have to be improved if losses were to be kept to an acceptable level of five percent or less, and bombing would have to be improved. Some satisfactory damage had been effected at Lille, and on several other raids, but bombing accuracy remained far from what was expected of daylight "precision" attacks.

After 9 October there were two changes in tactical alignment. The 14th Fighter Group went operational on P-38s, and the 92nd Bomb Group was pulled off operations, redesignated the 11 Combat Crew Replacement Center and became a training unit to supply new crews and crewmen to the other groups of the 1st Bomb Wing. Although training was its primary concern, it did on occasion take part in missions.

The weather turned bad in the last three weeks of October, and as a result the Eighth's heavies flew only one mission in that period. It was carried out on 21 October and opened a new phase in bomber operations, initiated at the urgent request of Allied naval officers.

They asked the Eighth to try and knock out the German U-Boat bases along the French coast — from whose sub pens enemy submarines were raising havoc with Allied shipping and posed a serious threat to the sea supply lines of the upcoming invasion of North Africa. The Eighth complied, and the base at Lorient was the first to be attacked.

On the 21st, 66 Fortresses and 24 Liberators were dispatched to Lorient with RAF and AAF fighters giving route escort, while 17 B-17s of 11 CCRC flew a diversion to Cherbourg. Nonetheless, the main force was intercepted by 36 enemy fighters when beyond its escort's range. The Luftwaffe shot down three B-17s and damaged six, while AAF gunners claimed 10-4-3.

Even as the air fighting took place, solid overcast in the target area turned all groups but the 97th back without bombing. The 97th persevered, however, and 15 of its planes dropped 30 2000-lb H.E. bombs from 17,500 feet. Their accuracy was extremely good. Half the bombs landed within 1000 feet of the MPI, two thirds within 2000 feet, and several direct hits were made on the roof of the central block of sub pen shelters but without penetration.

On 7 November, the 2nd Bomb Wing joined operations as its 44th Bomb Group flew the first mission for both organizations, sending seven B-24s on a diversionary sweep. The main bomber force, with which the 91st Bomb Group flew its first mission, made two separate attacks on Brest, four hours and thirteen minutes apart. In the first, 23 B-17s (8 from the 91st) got through deteriorating weather to bomb the sub pens and torpedo boat station in spite of intense and accurate flak. In the second, 11 B-24s of the 93rd Group struck at the sub pen docks. One Liberator was seriously damaged by the heavy flak but managed to return to England. Of the 199 bombs dropped, 36 landed within 2000 feet of the MPI. Sheds and part of a building were destroyed and two harbor craft were sunk.

Next day the Eighth returned to Lille, where 30 B-17s (301st and 306th) bombed the Fives-Lille works, while 11 B-17s of the 91st struck at Abbeville/Drucat. Both forces encountered numerous 190s and 109s with one B-17 of the 301st being lost to a combination of fighters and flak. Eleven German fighters were claimed shot down by the heavies.

A member of the Free French Resistance later reported: "On 8 November 1942, about 1220, about twenty planes appeared flying at 13,000 to 16,500 feet. At the time I was on the theater square. Several people around me shouted, 'There they are, I recognize the motors.' I noticed that the people were very calm and didn't even run to shelters. I should add that the alert was sounded after the bombs had fallen.

"A few minutes later, at about 1222, the Fives shop, the freight depot at the Lille railway station, and the tracks were hit by bombs. Immediately the antiaircraft guns began to fire, one plane was hit, and four aviators bailed out, landing at Marc en Baroeul. One of them was taken prisoner, and someone who saw him assured me that he was an American. Many people ran out to hide him and attacked the few officers and soldiers who had gone out to capture him.

"The occupants of the damaged plane had released their bombs before the plane crashed. Unfortunately, these fell on la Madeleine, the northeast suburbs of Lille, destroying about thirty houses and causing about fifteen casualties in Fontaine, Pasteur, Turenne and Abbe Lemire streets.

"About fifty bombs fell on the carpenter shop, the workshops and the foundry. This attack, and the bombing of 9 October last, have left intact only a third of the buildings of the factory."

After seventeen missions, the Eighth was clearly emerging as an effective force, but at this critical juncture its strength was suddenly sapped. From mid-September into November, it lost over half of its operational groups as they were needed and assigned elsewhere, along with other combat units under the Eighth's control. The culprit was TORCH.

OPERATION TORCH

As 1942 had progressed, the western Allies had been faced with the need to do something to relieve pressure on Russian forces in the East. A cross-Channel invasion was ruled out for the immediate future and the only alternative action which could be undertaken was GYMNAST. Consequently it was reinstated in July 1942 and renamed TORCH, an invasion of Northwest Africa to take place at three points.

The U.S. air contingent under TORCH was the Twelfth Air Force, undertaking the assignment for which the Eighth had originally been activated. The only way to get the Twelfth the number of groups it would need by the November date when TORCH would begin was to take units from the Eighth and add them to the eight groups in the U.S. which were available for assignment to the Twelfth. This was done, and between 14 September and 16 October fourteen units were transferred from the Eighth to the Twelfth — though some continued to serve the Eighth after the latter date. Included were the Eighth's two most experienced bomb groups and four of its five operational fighter groups.

```
        EIGHTH UNITS TRANSFERRED TO TWELFTH AIR FORCE

   ACTIVE UNITS              OPERATIONAL       MISSIONS/SORTIES

   97th Bomb Group          17 Aug - 21 Oct      15 Missions
   301st Bomb Group          5 Sep - 8 Nov        9 Missions
   15th Bomb Squadron        4 Jul - 2 Oct       48 Sorties
   1st Fighter Group        29 Aug - 25 Oct     273 Sorties
   14th Fighter Group       15 Oct - 21 Oct      74 Sorties
   31st Fighter Group        5 Aug - 9 Oct     1286 Sorties *
   52nd Fighter Group       24 Aug - 12 Sep      83 Sorties

   OTHER UNITS              TYPE     ASSIGNED     TRANSFERRED

   3rd Photo Group          F-4       5 Sep        16 Oct
   60th Troop Carrier Gp    C-47     12 Jun        14 Sep
   62nd Troop Carrier Gp    C-47      6 Sep        14 Sep
   64th Troop Carrier Gp    C-47     18 Aug        14 Sep
   81st Fighter Group       P-39      2 Oct        10 Oct
   82nd Fighter Group       P-38      2 Oct        10 Oct
   350th Fighter Group      P-39     Activated by VIII FC
                                     for Twelfth on 1 Oct,
                                     transferred same day.

        * During these sorties 31st claimed 2-3-4.
```

Beyond transferring fourteen units to the Twelfth, the Eighth Air Force also handled three Twelfth groups which flew the Atlantic and spent a short period in England before moving to North Africa. These were the 47th Bomb Group, the 310th Bomb Group and the 319th Bomb Group.

The Twelfth's units moved to North Africa between October 1942 and January 1943. With their removal from the Eighth and the beginning of the TORCH invasion of North Africa on 8 November 1942, the Eighth was left with only five operational groups — the 4th Fighter Group, and the 44th, 91st, 93rd and 306th Bomb Groups, which would be joined in action by the 303rd and 305th Bomb Groups on 17 November.

For the next six months these bomb groups would constitute the total striking power of the Eighth, but the two B-24 groups would not always be available or at full strength.

The travails and travels of the Liberator groups began even before TORCH. On its arrival in England, the 93rd BG was assigned to the 1st Bomb Wing and operated with the B-17 groups. Due to the difference in performance of the two types of bombers (the B-24s were faster and had trouble keeping their formation in place with the slower B-17s), it became apparent that B-17s and B-24s should operate separately. As a consequence several squadrons of the 93rd were assigned special duties, and then, on 5 December 1942, the Group was transferred to the 2nd Bomb Wing.

Between 25 October and 25 November, eight B-24s of the 93rd's 330th BS carried out anti-sub patrols over the Bay of Biscay under RAF Coastal Command. The Squadron operated on 19 days, flying 62 patrol sorties which resulted in the sighting of one sub and five enemy ships. On 11 November, a Liberator was engaged by five Ju 88s and claimed one destroyed and one probable without damage. On 21 November, another Liberator encountered five Me 210s, claiming two destroyed and one probable while sustaining only slight damage. One B-24 was lost due to weather on 29 October when it crashed, killing eleven crew members. Only one gunner survived.

From 22 through 24 November, the 409th BS operated six B-24s in the search for a Fortress missing over the Bay of Biscay. Thirteen sorties were flown during the three days, but the lost plane was never found. On the 22nd, three Liberators encountered enemy planes. One crew shot down an Arado Ar 196 and probably downed a Heinkel He 115, while the crew of another Liberator, attacked by three Ar 196s, claimed one destroyed and the other two damaged.

It was shortly after these operations that the 93rd was transferred to the 2nd Bomb Wing. But it was soon without its 329th Bomb Squadron. The Squadron was ordered to prepare for special intruder operations and moved to Bungay. At Bungay, from 14 December, it went into training for "Moling"— flights over enemy territory in bad weather to alert enemy air raid and defense establishments and interrupt enemy industrial production. After training and waiting for weather suitable for Moling, six missions of four to six aircraft were dispatched in the first two months of 1943, the first on 2 January. Unfortunately, in all cases the weather proved to be *too good* (i.e. the clouds broke up so the planes could not hide in them) and not a single sortie was completed. On 12 March 1943, the 329th resumed operations as part of the 93rd Bomb Group.

Meanwhile, on 7 December 1942, the air echelons of the 93rd's other three squadrons were sent to North Africa on detached service. There, flying from Tafaraoui and Gambut Main in support of TORCH, they carried out 23 missions, from 13 December through 20 February, before being sent back to England. In all, 274 aircraft were dispatched and 226 attacked, dropping 533 tons of bombs. Enemy aircraft were encountered on nine missions with gunners claiming 10-9-12. Five B-24s were lost to enemy action and three were lost operationally. One crashed into a mountain near Tafaraoui on arrival, one was washed out there while taxiing in excessive mud, and one was interned in Spanish Morocco.

While the 44th remained as the sole Liberator group in England, it was always under strength, having come across the Atlantic with three instead of four squadrons. Not until 22 March 1943 did a fourth squadron, the 506th, come overseas and join the 44th on operations.

A day after the first of the 93rd's planes began returning from North Africa, the 44th and 93rd put up their initial joint mission under the 2nd Bomb Wing. That day, 27 February, 14 of 15 B-24s dispatched by the two groups bombed sub pens at Brest without loss.

THE FOUR HORSEMEN

With the 93rd Group in North Africa for three months and the 44th Group at reduced strength, the main job of carrying forth the Eighth's bombing program after 8 November 1942 fell to the lot of its four Flying Fortress groups. These "Four Horsemen" thereupon blazed the way in bomber operations until fresh reinforcements arrived in England and entered action in May 1943. They extended their operations into Germany itself, and met and found ways to counter ever increasing Luftwaffe resistance to the incursion of American daylight bombers over Europe.

Following the opening of TORCH, the Eighth had flown two missions to the U-Boat base at St. Nazaire which was beyond the range of fighter escort — 31 B-17s and 12 B-24s bombing on the 9th, 15 B-17s and 9 B-24s bombing on the 14th. A third consecutive mission to St. Nazaire was undertaken on the 17th, employing Liberators of the 93rd (in the lead) and Fortresses of the 91st, 306th, 303rd and 305th — the Four Horsemen — with the latter two groups (the 305th on a diversion) flying their initial combat mission.

From 17 November 1942 through 4 May 1943, the Four Horsemen would fly all but one of the 35 Eighth missions — dispatching 2,558 aircraft of which 1,640 attacked and 68 flew diversions. For the same period, 617 Liberators would be dispatched on 32 missions with 208 attacking targets and 185 flying diversions. Combat losses for the period were 94 B-17s and 18 B-24s.

Beginning with the St. Nazaire mission of 23 November, German fighter tactics changed abruptly. Until then the majority of attacks on the heavies had been made from the rear, but that day nearly all attacks came form the front. The Germans had finally discovered the relative weakness of the B-17s (and B-24s) in forward firepower. It consisted of only a single handheld machine gun whose arc of fire left a blind spot which the upper turret could not cover. On this day, some fifty FW 190s pressed attacks from the front and shot down four Fortresses, two from the 91st.

The immediate remedy, beside adding two more handheld machine guns to the sides of the nose on B-17s, was to better coordinate groups and to improve the formations being flown, stacking planes so that some could cover the blind spots of others.

Until December, each group of the 1st Bomb Wing operated according to its own tactical doctrine. Thereafter, the groups were bound together in a more cohesive force by the tactical doctrine of the Wing, and the combat box formation was brought into being. With it, 18 to 21 bombers were stacked in such a way as to uncover as many of the top and bottom turrets as possible in order to bring the maximum fire to bear on the critical hemisphere of the attack (the forward hemisphere at this time). Later, three combat boxes were combined into the ultimate defensive formation, the combat wing.

At the same time formations were improved, bombing changed from individual aircraft bombing to element bombing, and then to squadron bombing, and finally to bombing by combat box. In this development, all bombardiers in a formation, instead of dropping their bombs individually, released their loads on the sighting of the lead plane — when the lead bombardier released his bombs, the others released theirs.

The new methods improved defensive capability and bombing accuracy, but at the same time the Luftwaffe increased its efforts to stop the American daylight bombers.

On 20 December, the Eighth sent 80 B-17s and 21 B-24s to attack the Luftwaffe repair depot at Romilly-sur-Seine. Located 65 miles SE of Paris, the depot was a high priority target which held the reserve aircraft of all types for the German Air Force in France and the Low Countries. The incoming bombers were met near the French coast, soon after their escort departed, by 60 enemy fighters from the Pas de Calais area. On approach to the target they encountered a further fifty 109s and 190s from the Paris-Evreux area, and on withdrawal had to fight off a second series of sorties by about half of the two forces. Two B-17s of the 91st were shot down near Rouen and one B-17 of the 306th was downed in the target area. On withdrawal, two more B-17s of the 306th were shot down, and finally a heavily damaged 303rd B-17 went down in the Channel. Bomber gunners claimed 53-13-8 enemy fighters, but actually they destroyed no more than 8 to 12 of the enemy's intercepting fighters.

Placement of additional handheld machine guns in nose of B-17F's as seen on planes of the 95th Bomb Group in mid-1943. "Impatient Virgin" was aircraft 42-3273. (Cliff Manella via Thomas M. Barnett)

The bombing by 60 Forts and 12 Libs had scored many direct hits on buildings and some on parked planes, and knocked out seven of eight AA batteries. The first bomb fell on the officers' mess, in which German officers were entertaining their ladies, and razed it to the ground.

On the next mission, back to the U-Boat bases on 30 December with Lorient as the target, fifty enemy fighters attacked the Fortresses. They operated in pairs and came in from all positions except astern. A 91st B-17 was shot down over Lorient. After the target, a 306th Fort inexplicably left the 305th formation it had tacked onto and was shot down. Its crew bailed out but were attacked by two 190s. A 305th B-17 then left its formation to protect the men in their parachutes, only to be shot down. Lone bombers out of formation did not last long against the 190s and 109s.

Both the ever present German flak and Luftwaffe fighters took their toll on the 3 January 1943 mission to St. Nazaire by 72 Forts and 13 Libs. The fighters struck in the target area when the bombers were beyond the range of their escort. Twenty 190s, operating with great skill and determination, carried out a series of vicious frontal attacks against the lead 303rd. In quick succession 3 of its planes were shot down.

Entering the bomb run, flak downed a fourth plane of the Group. Thirty plus fighters then hit the 91st which warded them off but lost a B-17 to flak over St. Nazaire. The 305th absorbed only a few fighter attacks but had 18 of its 21 planes damaged by flak. Behind it, the 306th met no fighters but lost one plane to flak and had five damaged. On withdrawal the 306th became separated and was hit by six 190s from Brest, which shot down one flak damaged B-17. Eight of thirteen 44th Liberators attacked without loss.

The bombing accomplished considerable fresh damage in the dock areas, and one or two direct hits were made on the reinforced concrete roof of the sub pens without penetration. This was about as well as could be done by the Eighth in attacks on the U-Boat bases, for the pens could not be breached by their bombs, but bomb damage to surrounding facilities could and did hinder submarine activity at the bases.

For the rest of January, bad weather, always a limiting factor to daylight operations, forced the Eighth to cancel a number of missions so that only four of fourteen planned missions were carried out in January. The second and third were to Lille and Lorient and cost the Eighth three and five bombers respectively. The fourth was something special.

Up to this point the Eighth had operated only over France and the Low Countries to a range of 225 miles from the English coast. Now, on 27 January 1943, it was ready to turn its attention to its main target, Germany, well beyond the range of its RAF fighter escort. Accordingly, the Eighth sent 64 Forts and 27 Libs out from England on a new route, over the North Sea, a route the Vikings had traversed when they came to England over a thousand years before. The planes had two targets. The B-17s were to hit Vegesack and the B-24s were to strike at Wilhelmshaven, 275 miles from the English coast. Only things didn't work out as expected.

Bad weather and then a navigational error made it impossible for the B-24s to locate their target, and they turned back. But not before German fighters intercepted them and shot down two of the Liberators. Of the Fortresses, 55 made it into Germany but found it impossible to attack Vegesack because of the weather. They thereupon turned for their secondary target, the dock area at Wilhelmshaven, and 53 dropped on that target, with the 306th Group being the first to drop bombs on German territory. Flak over the target, used to countering RAF night raids, was confused and ineffective. The B-17s suffered no losses to it, but lost one plane when they, too, were intercepted by enemy fighters. In all both forces withstood some 100 passes by 109s and 190s whose pilots, although determined, proved to be less experienced than those the bombers had encountered over France. Total bomber claims were 22-14-13, for the loss of three heavies. Besides the attack on Wilhelmshaven, two B-17s bombed the last resort target at Emden.

Although the mission was not executed as planned, it did hit Germany for the first time and proved that a small force of unescorted heavy bombers could penetrate the enemy homeland in daylight without suffering prohibitive losses. The stage was thus set for more and bigger raids on Germany.

In February weather again hampered operations, and Eighth bombers flew but seven missions, only five of which resulted in the bombing of enemy targets. On the 2nd, 4th and 14th, the heavies were dispatched to strike the marshalling yards at Hamm in the Ruhr. On the first and last of these missions, weather forced the planes to return without bombing. On 4 February, however, 39 of the 65 Forts dispatched bombed the industrial area at Emden, their secondary target. There they stirred up a hornet's nest of enemy fighters. Most were Me 109s and FW 190s, while for the first time the Eighth was opposed by twin engine fighters, Me 110s and Ju 88s. In the resulting air action four Fortresses were shot down and another lost to flak.

On 26 February, the Four Horsemen and 17 B-24s set out for Bremen, but clouds obscured the target and the bombers had to attack Wilhelmshaven instead. They drew some sixty single engine and ten twin engine fighters. The German pilots pressed their attacks with determination, though they did not come in so consistently from the front. In the ensuing battle four B-17s and two B-24s were shot down and one B-17 was lost to flak.

Next day, on a mission to the U-Boat base at Brest, the RAF provided escort of such quality that the 60 attacking bombers saw only ten FW 190s and suffered no loss.

The Four Horsemen tried for Hamm again on 4 March, as 14 B-24s flew a diversion, but once more weather interferred. Three groups turned back, with 28 planes of two groups bombing the Wilton Ship Yard at Rotterdam. Fifteen planes of the 91st Group, separated from the others, plunged on through the clouds and emerged into clear weather quite alone. Unhesitatingly the 91st continued, reached the marshalling yards and bombed with unusual accuracy. But when it turned for home the lone group was engaged in a running fight with some fifty Me 109s, FW 190s and Me 110s. As the bombers headed for the clouds again one heavy fighter attack was launched from them. The Group did its best to evade the enemy by diving, climbing and turning into attacks, then for awhile it was safe in the clouds. But when the cloud cover fell behind and the coast was neared, there were so many enemy fighters about that further evasive action only led the formation from the path of one flight of fighters into the path of another. To make matters even worse, the Group had to reduce speed to help cover damaged aircraft.

When at last the coast was reached and the attacks let up, except for a few 110s which persisted part way back across the water, three Forts had been shot down. A fourth ditched in the Channel with seven of its crew being rescued. All eleven other aircraft were damaged, one being a total loss and four requiring major repairs. Claims were 13-3-4. Remarkably, a lone group had survived over Germany and fought its way home in spite of large numbers of enemy fighters.

The Luftwaffe worked a new gambit on 8 March. The B-24 formation that day (sixteen planes of the 44th and 93rd) was sent to bomb the marshalling yards at Rouen, flying alone but heavily escorted by RAF Spitfires. As the Libs reached the IP, a gruppe of 190s went for the Spitfire escort, fully occupying its attention. Then another gruppe of 190s went for the uncovered B-24s. They hit with ferocity on the bomb run and shot down the lead plane, quite disrupting the bombing so that the bombs fell two miles north of the yards. The fighter attacks continued to the coast, downing a second B-24. A third was so damaged it crash landed in England. Liberator claims were 14-3-3.

On 18 March, the U-Boat yards at Vegesack were again the target, and this time the heavies got through with 73 B-17s and 24 B-24s bombing. The route was carefully planned, and

**Consolidated B-24D, 41-23819, of the 44th Bomb Group early in 1943, with the group insignia visible on the nose. (AAF)**

the bombers did not meet opposition until near Heligoland, but from there to the target and sixty miles out to sea on the return they were engaged by 50 to 60 fighters. However, these seemed to be new units lacking in skill for only one Fort and one Lib were lost. Gunner claims, though, went sky high to 52-20-23, a total almost twice the number of enemy fighters engaged. Still a sizeable number of German fighters were shot down, and the bombing had been very accurate.

With nine of ten missions completed, March had been the Eighth's biggest operational month so far. With the Four Horsemen bearing the brunt of the action, three times the primary target had been in Germany, five times in France and once in Holland. In April weather again reduced operations, and the heavies completed only four missions, two to France, one to Belgium and one to Bremen. During these missions, German battle tactics continued to evolve.

On 4 April, while 26 B-24s flew a diversion, the Four Horsemen dispatched 97 Fortresses to bomb the Renault motor vehicle works at Billancourt near Paris. Eighty-five planes dropped 251 tons of bombs with excellent result, heavily damaging all major buildings and reducing production for five months. While over the target unescorted the B-17s were heavily engaged by 50 to 75 fighters and lost four bombers. The enemy concentrated on frontal attacks and for the first time made a number of coordinated attacks, executed by four to seven aircraft approaching from the front in waves with 1,000 to 1,500 yards between them. In another switch in tactics the Germans began concentrating their attacks on the most unprotected squadron of a combat wing. On this occasion they went for the low squadron of one wing and shot down three of its six planes.

Of the day's events French sources reported: "Two Flying Fortresses crashed near the village of Notre Dame du Vaudreuil in Normandy. They were flying in the rear of their formation pursued by twenty 190s. One Fortress was hit under the left wing, broke into flames and fell very rapidly. One man only had time to bail out. The second plane destroyed four German planes, which crashed in the district, before being itself destroyed. Ten men were able to bail out."

The Eighth's last mission of the month was flown to the Focke Wulf factory at Bremen on 17 April, 115 Four Horsemen taking off and 106, in two combat wing formations, attacking. The bombing was highly accurate despite flak and violent fighter opposition, but it was all for nought. Unknown to intelligence the FW factory had been out of production for six months! But the real story of the raid was the resulting air battle.

Up to 150 German fighters had been assembled in defense of the target after a German observation plane reported the B-17s over the North Sea an hour before their arrival. They struck as the two (54-plane) combat wings slid into trail formation by combat boxes for bombing, and singled out the first combat wing whose formation was loose and vulnerable. The enemy fighters concentrated on the leading 91st Group box from the front, even flying through their own flak in an attempt to disrupt bombing. Then on withdrawal the fighters attacked constantly from all directions until the Forts were past the Frisian Islands. As a result of the vicious attacks all six planes of the low squadron of the leading 91st were shot down, while the 306th Group, which made up the first combat wing with the 91st, had nine of its B-17s shot down and lost a tenth to flak. The second combat wing, which maintained a tight formation throughout, suffered no losses. However, the 16 bombers lost that day marked the heaviest loss the Eighth had yet sustained. The gunners also hit a high mark, claiming 62-15-17 enemy planes, although in fact they accounted for only ten German fighters.

It was an ill-starred day for the Eighth, but it was not a set back. Operations would continue *and* expand. And already the Eighth had fashioned one major accomplishment.

At the start of 1943, the Luftwaffe had only some 300 fighters in the West. By mid-year it had some 600. The Eighth was forcing the hard pressed Luftwaffe to cut back elsewhere and rush planes to the West to try and stop it. And in doing that it was accomplishing more to end the war than (so far) it was with its bombing, even though the bombing, especially of Germany itself, was the catalyst which forced the Germans to redeploy their aircraft. Its next job, already begun, would be to destroy those enemy fighters in the air — just as they, in reverse, were attempting to destroy the Eighth's planes.

To this end, the Luftwaffe was still refining its tactics, seeking the sure way to annihilate the day bombers. Its deadly nose attacks had been effectively countered, but in their place emerged a Pandora's box of assorted ills. Coordinated fighter attacks were fruitful and infinitely variable; twin engine fighters promised greater success with their heavier firepower; parachute mines were dropped on the bomber formations; air to air bombing was attempted; and plans were underway for the use of rockets.

As Bremen on 17 April had proved, the Eighth was in for an ever tougher time when its bombers were beyond fighter escort range. And it was clear that what was needed most were longer ranging escort fighters. They were a must, and already the first of them were on the scene.

For the first three months of 1943 the Spitfire equipped 4th was the only Eighth fighter group. It operated on 67 days in that period, always limited by the short range of its Spitfires. Then in March it began to convert to the Republic P-47C Thunderbolt, which had a considerably increased range over the Spitfire. It could give escort along the way to and from German targets but could not, at first, escort the heavies beyond the German border.

As the 4th converted to this new fighter, two new groups, the 56th and 78th Fighter Groups, were readying for combat with their own P-47C's. Their first operation came on 8 April and was merely a Rodeo on which 56th and 78th P-47s joined P-47s of the 4th, 23 in all carrying it out without undue incident. The Thunderbolt had arrived.

Five days later, 13 April, the first full missions for the two new groups were flown. In the morning, with two 4th squadrons of P-47s leading a dozen 78th Thunderbolts, a 36-plane Ramrod (an escort for bombers attacking targets in the Occupied Countries) was flown. Later in the day all three groups put up one squadron each in sending 40 P-47s on a Rodeo. The planes made landfall in near Le Touquet at 31,000 feet, swept over St. Omer and made landfall out at Dunkirk without encountering anything more than some inaccurate heavy flak near Dunkirk. The only untoward incident occurred when a P-47 of the 56th flown by Capt. Roger B. Dyar had its engine cut out over Dunkirk. Keeping his head, Dyar put the plane into a glide and managed to get back across the Channel, coming in over the coast at 1,000 feet and landing five miles in at Deal.

On 15 April, the three groups sent 59 Thunderbolts out on

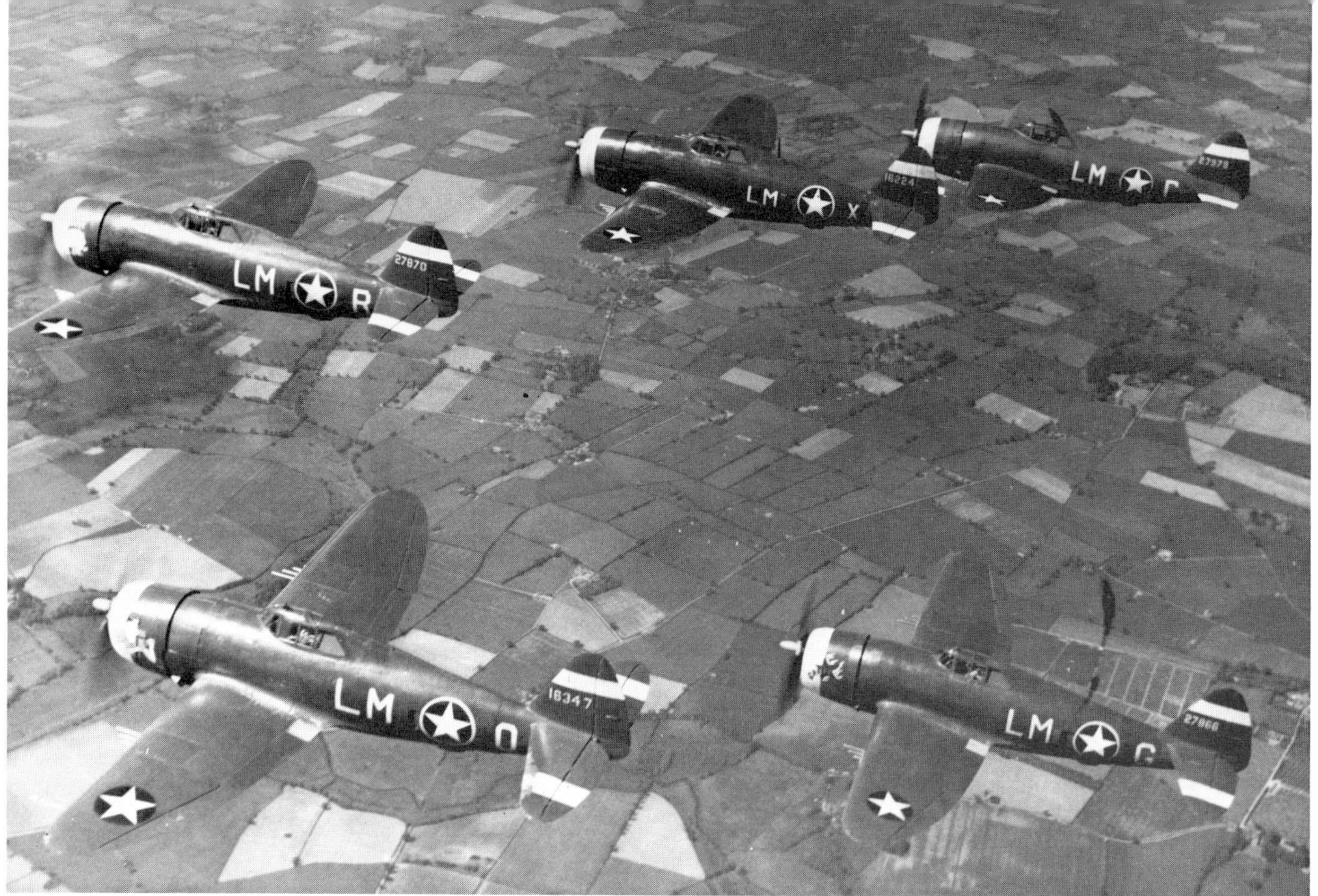

**Republic P-47C's (second and third planes) and P-47D's of the 56th Fighter Group flying over England in mid-1943. (AAF)**

a Rodeo, and the P-47 drew blood for the first time. Over the coast of France, Major Don Blakeslee (C.O. of the 4th's 335th FS) led ten P-47s in a dive on three FW 190s, lined up on one and shot it down to crash into an Ostend backyard. In further action two other 4th pilots each claimed a 190 destroyed, while one 4th pilot was shot down. Three for one was a good start, but two additional P-47s failed to return, having gone down due to engine failure.

BUILD-UP

The days of the Four Horsemen ended in early May as at last the Eighth began receiving major reinforcements in bomber aircraft. One new unit going into action in May was the 322nd Bomb Group (Medium), equipped with Martin B-26B Marauders. It had come over in December 1942 and had been assigned to the new 3rd Bomb Wing, which was now to begin carrying out raids against enemy targets in Occupied Europe. In May and June it was joined in the U.K. by three other B-26 groups — the 323rd, 386th and 387th Bomb Groups.

No less than five new B-17 equipped heavy groups arrived in England during May. The first three — the 94th, 95th and 96th Bomb Groups — were assigned to yet another new wing, the 4th Bomb Wing, and immediately went into operation with it. The two other new groups — the 351st and 379th Bomb Groups — were assigned to the 1st Bomb Wing, and they joined the Four Horsemen on operations before the end of the month. Also, the 92nd Bomb Group (11 CCRC since November) was returned to action on 14 May 1943 assigned also to the 1st Bomb Wing.

Unlike the original build-up in England in 1942, this build-up would continue. From June through September, six more

B-17 groups and two new B-24 groups would join operations, while three new Thunderbolt equipped fighter groups would go into action during August and September.

On 13 May, the 1st Bomb Wing's Four Horsemen returned to a familiar target, Meaulte, with 124 P-47s giving route escort. And this time, despite enemy fighter attacks which cost them three bombers, they finished the repair depot for good, dropping 218 tons of bombs with great accuracy. Behind the veterans, the 4th Bomb Wing flew its initial mission to the fighter field at St. Omer/Longuenesse, sending out 72 B-17s of the 94th, 95th and 96th Groups with RAF escort. Thirty-one Forts of the first two groups bombed the target, and scored a clean miss. The 96th, unable to form up in time, turned back over the Channel, but lost one plane when it had to ditch due to mechanical failure.

Next day, the Eighth put up its maximum force (dispatching 236 bombers and 118 fighters) as part of a combined attack with the RAF against the German war machine. The RAF, on the night of 13/14 May, attacked Bochum in the Ruhr (298 planes dropping 1198 tons), Pilsen in Czechoslovakia (141 planes dropping 527 tons) and Berlin. The Eighth then sent its 1st and 2nd Bomb Wings to bomb shipyards at Kiel by day, with 109 B-17s and 17 B-24s dropping 293 tons at 1205 hours with good results. The Kiel mission required a flight of 460 miles and caught the enemy's defenses somewhat unprepared, although 120 enemy fighters did rise to give combat. Only 3 Forts were lost, but enemy fighters zeroed in on the small Liberator formation at the back, downing 5 B-24s.

To the south, the Eighth sent the new 4th Bomb Wing to hit the Ford and General Motors plants at Antwerp, and Courtrai airfield in Belgium. At Antwerp, 38 B-17s of the

15

94th and 95th Groups dropped 91 tons at 1320 hours with very good results (45 hits at the Ford plant). The 96th and 351st Groups (the latter, of the 1st Bomb Wing, on its first mission) hit Courtrai with 34 Fortresses at 1230 hours. One B-17 was lost at Antwerp, two at Courtrai.

A total of 118 P-47s were sent out on fighter sweeps over Belgium and France and to provide escort for the attack on Antwerp. A number of enemy fighters, mainly FW 190s, were encountered, and the P-47s successfully prevented many potential attacks against the bombers. For the day the Thunderbolts claimed 4-6-11, and three P-47s failed to return.

One of the P-47 victories was scored by a wing leader who reported: "I was leading the Wing and trailing above the bombers at 28,000 feet when I saw eight enemy fighters going in to attack the bombers from one o'clock, breaking upwards. I led one section down over the front of the leading section of the bombers and did a slight port turn, when I saw an FW 190 break up and under me. The FW 190 half rolled and went home. I sighted a queue of about eight enemy planes forming up to the right and 1,000 feet below the bombers. I turned and went down with the section to divert the enemy formation, and as I did they turned into us. I then completed a starboard turn and chased two enemy aircraft who were starting to attack the rear box of bombers. I overtook them rapidly in a diving attack. I fired a very short burst at the No. 2 enemy fighter from 75 yards, saw strikes on the tail and passed over it, opening fire on the No. 1 plane from 150 yards and 45 degrees from its port side. I saw strikes on the fuselage, the cockpit hood fly off, and black and white smoke pouring from the aircraft as it dove to the left."

There was one other Eighth action on 14 May. The 3rd Bomb Wing flew its first mission, sending twelve B-26s of the 322nd Group to hit an electric power station at Ijmuiden in Holland. One Marauder aborted, and eleven carried out the attack flying unescorted to the target at 50 feet and dropping delayed action bombs from 100 feet at 1100 hours. The bombing was ineffective, as only a few bombs hit the target while others went wide and some did not detonate. On return, the planes scattered, flew too high and so came under fire from flak, and almost all were damaged with seven men wounded. Back over England, after the rest of its crew bailed out, one plane crashed killing its pilot. The B-26s had made a rough start at low altitude attack, which was not endearing itself to the crews, but far worse was to come.

Three days later, while the heavies went south to targets in France, the Marauders of the 322nd flew their second low level mission. It was also to be their last. Eleven B-26s were sent out, and again the target was the electric power station at Ijmuiden, plus a similar target at Haarlem. Over the North Sea one B-26 aborted due to generator trouble and returned to base. The ten remaining planes continued on and reached the coast but at the wrong spot. They flew head on into a vicious barrage of antiaircraft fire, and the lead bomber and one other were quickly shot down. Two other B-26s collided and went smashing into the ground, while yet another succumbed to damage and force landed in Holland.

Five were still left and they continued on, hopelessly off course, flew into the Amsterdam area, bombed a station there, and were riddled by flak. Three of these planes went down from damage one after another off the coast, and the other two were shot down into the North Sea by Me 109s. Two gunners from one of the latter crews were picked up five days later by a British destroyer. Eleven planes had been sent out, one aborted and ten were lost — two crewmen were rescued and twenty others survived as prisoners of war from the planes shot down in Holland.

It was a disaster, which quickly resulted in the Marauders being taken off operations. In the following two months, the 322nd Group, and also the arriving 323rd, 386th and 387th Groups, were held out of action, placed under VIII Air Support Command (in June) and trained to become part of a tactical air force.

While the Marauders went through hell in Holland on the 17th, 159 B-17s (100 of the 1st Wing and 59 of the 4th Wing) were sent to attack the sub pens and port area at Lorient, while 39 B-24s went out to bomb the U-Boat station at Bordeaux. In the first of these missions, 80 Forts dropped 198 tons on the sub pens and 38 dropped 92 tons on the power station. Some forty enemy aircraft, mostly 190s, intercepted and after sizing up matters began a series of stern attacks on the high squadron of the last group attacking the sub pens, the 305th, shooting down four of its planes. In all 6 Fortresses were lost (two by the 4th Wing) while the bombers claimed 27 enemy fighters shot down.

At Bordeaux, in an all B-24 attack, 34 Libs dropped 86 tons with high accuracy, creating great damage including the breaching of the locks of the sub basin. No planes were lost at the target, but on approaching the French coast on the way to Bordeaux one B-24 had left the formation and headed toward France. It was never seen again.

In the six weeks following 17 May, the Eighth Air Force went to targets in Germany six times and to targets in France six times in the course of a dozen missions. On 29 May, six B-17s were lost over Rennes, mainly to some 70 enemy fight-

**Martin B-26B Marauders of the 322nd Bomb Group with 41-31671, "Buddy's REBEL" in foreground. (Col. Robert W. Keller)**

**Battle damage from 20 mm cannon hits to B-24D at Kiel, 14 May, and to B-17F at Lorient, 17 May 1943. (Impact)**

ers, and eight B-17s were lost over St. Nazaire, mainly to the intense flak there.

At St. Nazaire, the Boeing YB-40 put in its initial appearance. It was a heavily armed B-17F (two top turrets, a chin turret and double guns at the waist positions plus an extra load of ammunition and no bombs) designed as a powerful "escort cruiser" to other Forts. The 327th BS of the 92nd BG had twelve of them and flew them on missions through July in the most vulnerable spots to protect other Fortresses. The concept did not work out with any real measure of success — the heavier YB-40s could not keep up with the standard B-17F, and German fighter pilots quickly learned to avoid them — and the planes were withdrawn from action. The YB-40s did leave the Eighth one legacy — the chin turret. which was soon made standard on the B-17G Fortress.

On 11 June, the Eighth sent 252 heavies to Bremen. They were thwarted by weather and bombed U-Boat yards at Wilhelmshaven and the port at Cuxhaven. The mission was countered by 125 enemy fighters, and eight bombers failed to return.

The 1st Bomb Wing was sent to Bremen again on 13 June, and made it, while 76 B-17s of the 4th Bomb Wing headed for Kiel. U-Boat yards were the targets in both cases. Bombing by 102 Forts was fairly good at Bremen and 4 B-17s were lost. At Kiel, 60 B-17s ran into some 200 enemy fighters which spoiled the bombing and nearly annihilated the leading 95th Group. It lost 10 of its 16 attacking aircraft. Then over the Channel on return, the 94th Group, with many guns unmanned, was suddenly hit by twelve Ju 88s. These night fighters swiftly knocked down 9 of the Group's bombers, bringing the day's losses by the 4th Bomb Wing to 22 Forts. That made it 26 Fortresses lost in one day — 21 to enemy aircraft, 2 to flak, 1 by collision with another B-17, and 2 to unknown causes — the heaviest blow yet suffered by the Eighth. Claims of 41-7-15 did little to ease the blow.

While 42 Forts went to Antwerp on 22 June, 235 were sent to attack the synthetic rubber plant at Huls in the Ruhr, which accounted for thirty percent of German rubber production. Of 422 tons dropped on the plant, 88.6 tons were on target. All buildings were hit, there were 186 dead and 500 wounded, and it would take forty days to regain one third production. Some 125 German fighters were encountered, and the Fortresses lost 16 planes (including one of eleven YB-40s on the mission to flak) while claiming 46-21-35.

An intelligence report from Germany subsequently stated that one Luftwaffe fighter gruppe had 42 planes and 45 pilots before the Huls mission. After it, the gruppe had 17 planes serviceable and 20 pilots.

On 25 June, 275 B-17s were dispatched to attack targets at Bremen and Hamburg, but heavy clouds broke up the mission. Nonetheless, 149 dropped on estimated location from 27,500 feet, and 18 attacked a German convoy, possibly hitting one ship. Eighteen bombers failed to return.

During the mission, several enemy operated B-17s were reported. One of these was sighted below one group for five minutes, then it pulled out and headed for the German coast unmolested by enemy fighters. Another shot off two green flares, crossed in front of a group and joined it on the right. And another "unidentified B-17" flew back and forth through one formation just off the English coast.

From 10 June 1943, the Eighth operated under the Combined Bomber Offensive directive (delineating target priorities), stemming from the Combined Chiefs of Staff. The directive was a result of the Casablanca Conference held in January 1943, which established Anglo-American policies for Europe (including HUSKY, an invasion of Sicily), the Far East and Pacific. The CBO Plan specified the following target systems to be attacked and destroyed by the Eighth Air Force:

1) Intermediate objective:
   German fighter strength.
2) Primary objectives:
   German submarine yards and bases.
   Remainder of the German aircraft industry.
   Ball bearings.
   Oil (Contingent upon attacks against the Ploesti oil fields from the Mediterranean).
3) Secondary objectives:
   Synthetic rubber and tires.
   Military motor transport vehicles.

These target systems became key objectives for the Eighth's bombers in the months to come. But as results would eventually show, oil was rated too low.

HUSKY, the invasion of Sicily established at the Casablanca Conference, also effected the Eighth Air Force. Once again its Liberators were needed in the Mediterranean — to add their strength to the B-24s of the Ninth Air Force in strategic attacks in support of HUSKY, scheduled for 10 July 1943,

```
     LIBERATOR OPERATIONS IN THE MEDITERRANEAN
            2 July 1943 - 21 August 1943

              A/C Dis-  A/C At-   Bomb   A/C   Claims
              patched   tacking   Tons   Lost  of E/A

HUSKY *         660       598     1602    14    54-8-?

TIDALWAVE       103        98             30    17-0-?

Post-Husky      227       196      368    10    50-4-?

* 93rd and 44th flew 10 missions, 389th 6 missions.
```

and to take part in TIDALWAVE, a very special low level mission against the Ploesti oil fields.

As a result, the 93rd and 44th Groups were pulled off operations in mid-June and, along with the newly arrived and not yet operational 389th Bomb Group, sent to the Benghazi area in Libya. The first two departed on 26 and 27 June with 39 and 38 aircraft respectively, and the first mission was flown on 2 July against airfields in Italy. The 389th flew its initial mission on 9 July. In all ten missions against airfields and rail communications were flown through 19 July. Thereafter the groups trained for TIDALWAVE and carried it out in conjunction with the Ninth's two Lib groups on 1 August 1943, attacking Ploesti in one of the most famous missions of the war. After Ploesti, four "Post-Husky" missions were flown — to Wiener Neustadt on 13 August, to Foggia airfields on 16 August, to the Foggia marshalling yards on 19 August, and to the Cancello depot and marshalling yards on 21 August. Then the three groups headed back to England and were "at home" again by 29 August. In all during their sojurn in the Med, they had dispatched 990 aircraft of which 892 attacked. Losses amounted to 54 bombers. Gunner claims were 121-12-35. A total of 420 men were MIA, 28 were KIA and 88 wounded. The three Eighth Liberator groups had done a fine job, but at a considerable cost.

Meanwhile, as weather allowed, Eighth operations were continued from England by the thirteen groups of B-17s operational at the start of July. On 14 July, while seven Fortress groups attacked airfields at Le Bourget and Amiens, six other Fortress groups hit Villacoublay, where the Luftwaffe had its main servicing and repair depot for FW 190s. There, 96 B-17s (accompanied by five YB-40s) dropped 233 tons of bombs from 22,000 to 25,000 feet.

Next day a report from Switzerland stated: "Results of bombing Villacoublay very successful. Following virtually destroyed: the Junkers works which had an output of about 12 Ju 52s per month. Partially destroyed: hangars along the National Road 186 and FW hangars. The number of aircraft destroyed is very large. A considerable number of 190s in Bievres Wood were destroyed by fire. About 100 German airmen were killed."

The Eighth's B-26 medium bombers resumed operations on 16 July, now under VIII Air Support Command, as 14 bombed the Abbeville marshalling yard while others flew a diversion. It was the first mission for the 323rd Bomb Group. The 322nd resumed ops on 31 July, while the 386th went operational on 30 July and the 387th on 15 August. The mediums would fly 283 sorties in July, 1,190 in August and 3,033 in September, claiming 20-10-11 enemy aircraft during the three months and losing 13 Marauders in action.

On 17 July, a mission by 332 B-17s to an aircraft factory in Amsterdam was almost completely thwarted by weather, but this did not keep the Germans from attempting one special effort to stop the bombers. Over Heligoland a Fortress formation was bombed extensively by Ju 88s which flew 1,000 feet above it. One B-17 was seen to explode when an aerial bomb went off near the waist window, and five other B-17s received damage due to bomb fragments. The lost B-17 was one of only two bombers failing to return that day.

Throughout the first half of 1943, poor and bad weather over Germany consistently limited Eighth operations to German targets. However, forecasters predicted a period of good weather for the last week in July, and as a result the Eighth prepared to join with the RAF in round the clock combined attacks against key points in Germany, with Hamburg being the main joint target.

The first of these operations was set for 24 July, but the weather over Germany was not ready to cooperate. Therefore, a full force of 324 B-17s was ordered to head north to three targets in Norway. The bombers, after making nearly blind takeoffs, climbed through the solid overcast covering England and assembled over splasher beacons. All but fifteen accomplished assembly, and 309 headed for Norway in three forces. The smallest had the longest mission yet undertaken (a 1900 mile round trip) and managed to get 41 planes through to bomb the submarine workshops and harbor installations at Trondheim — causing severe damage in the port area and sinking the sub U-122 and a 1500 ton cargo vessel.

The largest force scored 151 direct hits on the magnesium, aluminum and nitrate works at Heroya, 70 miles SW of Oslo, almost completely destroying them. One attacking plane was damaged by flak and headed for neutral Sweden. It landed wheels up in a bog at Vannacka — the first of 131 Eighth Air Force bombers which would come down in Sweden during the war. The third force, sent to the sub base at Bergen, found its target cloud covered and returned without bombing, two of its planes slightly damaged by flak.

```
            COMBINED ATTACKS   24 to 30 JULY 1943

DATE    TARGET           DIS   ATT   TONS   LOST    CLAIMS

24th    Heroya           180   167   414     1  )
        Trondheim         45    41    79     0  )   13-4-3
        Bergen            84     0     0     0

24/25   RAF - Hamburg    791   740   2300   12

25th    Hamburg    )            68   156 )
        Kiel       )     323    67   168 )   19     44-6-27
        Warnemunde )            26    65 )
        T/O's                   57   131 )

25/26   RAF - Essen      705   599   1948   24

26th    Hamburg    )            54   129   14  )
        Hannover   )     303    92   243   10  )  60-10-36
        T/O's                   53   131    0  )

27/28   RAF - Hamburg    787   739   2313   17

28th    Kassel           182    49   119    7      26-15-23
        T/O's                    7    13    0
        Oschersleben     120    28    68   15      56-19-41
        T/O's                   11    22    0

        VIII FC  ----    105                 1       9-1-6

29th    Kiel       )            91   208 )
        Warnemunde )     249    54   119 ) 10       48-8-33
        T/O's                   48   108 )

29/30   RAF - Hamburg    777   726   2277   28

30th    Kassel           119    94         12  )
        Kassel            67    37   305     0  )  48-13-32
        T/O's                    3     7     0  )

        VIII FC  ----    107                 7      25-4-8
```

Weather improved over Germany after the 24th, and the Eighth dispatched more than 300 heavies on each of the next two days to targets in Germany. But on both occasions heavy clouds forced a number of planes to abort or seek targets of opportunity. On the 25th, Hamburg U-Boat yards were attacked despite heavy smoke from the previous night's RAF raid; Kiel U-Boat yards were effectively hit although there was strong fighter resistance and intense flak; and the Heinkel factory at Warnemunde was accurately bombed. Next day, U-Boat yards at Hamburg and the synthetic rubber plant at Hannover were the primary targets, hit with good and fair results. Some forty and eighty enemy fighters were encountered. Thirteen bombers were lost to enemy aircraft, seven to flak and four to unknown causes.

On 28 July, over 300 heavies were again sent out to Germany. Targets were a Fieseler FW 190 parts factory at Kassel (two wings were turned back by a weather front extending to 30,000 feet and one wing got through) and the AGO FW 190 plant at Oschersleben in the deepest penetration of Germany yet made (with most of the force turned back by towering cumulus clouds). Bombing was fair and very good respectively. Intensive opposition by over 100 fighters was met at both targets. At Oschersleben, 109s and 190s used cloud cover to initiate attacks, dove just before getting into range of the B-17s' nose guns, pulled up and attacked the undersides of the B-17s. Parachute bombs and air to air bombing were responsible for the loss of three B-17s when one received a direct hit and crashed into two others. In all, 22 Fortresses were lost, and the results would have been worse but for an important new development — P-47s met the bombers over Germany on their way out.

That day, for the first time, the Eighth's P-47D's used droppable belly fuel tanks to increase their escort range. These were paper ferry tanks of 200 gallon capacity and unpressurized. Fuel could not be extracted from them above 22,000 feet, so they were used to that altitude and then dropped. They extended escort range to a radius of 265 miles. Later, pressurized drop tanks of 108 gallon capacity were used, extending escort range to 350 miles.

With their belly tanks (affectionately called "babies") 41 P-47s of the 4th FG were able to penetrate Germany on 28 July and come to the aid of the B-17s while they were under heavy fighter attack. The Thunderbolts charged into 45 to 60 enemy fighters preying on the bombers and shot down six 109s and three 190s, probably destroyed a 109, and damaged four 190s and two 109s, for the loss of only one P-47. The 78th's P-47s did not make contact with the enemy, but nonetheless it was a good beginning for improved and more effective operations.

Continuing combined attacks and strikes at top CBO targets, the Eighth hit the U-Boat yards at Kiel and the Heinkel factory producing FW 190 parts at Warnemunde on 29 July, and two Fieseler factories producing FW 190 parts at Kassel on 30 July. On both days, losses were much lower than on the preceding days. The reason on the 30th was again the intervention of withdrawal escort P-47s using belly tanks. They

**B-17F Fortresses of the 95th Bomb Group, 334th Bomb Squadron top and 412th Bomb Squadron below, fly in formation on the way to their target in Norway. (AAF)**

found the B-17s returning from Kassel under heavy attack by up to two hundred enemy fighters.

The 78th FG circled over the bombers to engage some 100 enemy fighters which were attacking or preparing to attack the Forts. They were in groups of two and four, and there were many single aircraft. Few of the enemy pilots took evasive action, even when attacked from above or the side, as they were engrossed in lining up on the bombers and did not at first consider the P-47s as anything but friendly aircraft. Maj. Eugene Roberts positioned his flight to the side and below the bombers as the enemy fighters lined up to make head-on attacks. Then when an enemy fighter passed, he got behind it, tipped upward and fired. He then slid out and, when another enemy fighter passed, got behind it and repeated the process, destroying in this way two 190s and a 109, and becoming the first Eighth fighter pilot to score a triple. Total 78th claims were 16-2-4; losses were 3 P-47s and pilots.

One squadron of the 56th FG maneuvered into position to the left of the bombers and one to the right while 60 Me 109s and FW 190s were making attacks. These were pressed home aggressively from above and to the side of the bombers, with a 180 degree turn being made to the front, followed by frontal attacks in a forty-five degree dive. The 56th soon found that making a pass at the enemy fighters as they dove at the bombers caused them to increase the angle of their dive and break off the attack, going under the bombers and then climbing into position for another try. The 56th's pilots also climbed back into their former position and were thus able to ward off several attacks by using the same tactics. Total claims for the 56th were 4-2-2 for the loss of two P-47s and their pilots.

The 4th FG found over 150 Me's and FW's attacking the bombers when it arrived on the scene. The enemy fighters were making attacks by diving steeply down from the sun, slightly to the rear, attacking, and then flicking over and diving away. The 4th Group's Thunderbolts jumped them as they went down into their attacks and claimed 5-0-2 for the loss of two P-47s and their pilots.

The 30th of July was the climax of the week of combined attacks in which the Eighth significantly improved its escort capability and, as never before, operated with strength and continuity to deliver its heaviest blows yet against the enemy. It was a week which promised that the German war machine would sustain even greater blows in the immediate future, and led directly to the great and bloody air battle which took place over Germany on the first anniversary of Eighth Air Force operations.

REGENSBURG AND SCHWEINFURT, AND STARKEY

By the first half of August, VIII Bomber Command's strength in heavy bomber units had grown to sixteen groups of B-17s (nine in the 1st Bomb Wing and seven in the 4th Bomb Wing) and three groups of B-24s (which were then carrying out Post-Husky operations in the Mediterranean). It would receive only one more heavy group by November. Thus it was to be mainly the sixteen Fortress groups to whose lot would fall the task of meeting the Luftwaffe's greatest efforts in August and October to so smash the Eighth's heavies that they would be forced to halt their ever more damaging campaign of daylight precision bombing against Germany.

Following 30 July, the Eighth's B-17s recuperated for a dozen days before flying three effective missions on the 12th, 15th and 16th of August. Then the Eighth prepared for its greatest and deepest mission so far, to be carried out on the anniversary of its first raid over Europe. This would be a two pronged attack into Germany, with the targets being the Messerschmitt Me 109 production center at Regensburg, and the heart of German ball bearing production at Schweinfurt.

The 1st Bomb Wing (to Schweinfurt) and the 4th Bomb Wing (to Regensburg) were to be dispatched together. They would cross into Europe with the fullest possible protection from the Eighth's four P-47 groups and the RAF's Spitfires, and then, well over Germany, diverge to strike their respective targets. After bombing, the 4th Bomb Wing would not return to England but would fly on to bases in North Africa. This was planned on the assumption it would be a safer way of withdrawal and was made possible by the fact the B-17s of the 4th Wing all were equipped with long range fuel tanks. The 1st Bomb Wing (not having such tanks) would return to England after bombing and be picked up as it departed Germany by the fullest possible P-47 and Spit withdrawal escort.

Only things didn't work out exactly that way. That old bugaboo weather saw to it.

On the morning of 17 August 1943, the day of the great mission, bad weather over its bases prevented the 1st Wing's heavies from taking off until three and a half hours later than planned. The 4th Wing's fields were not in as bad shape, and its planes had to get off on time in order to reach unfamiliar North Africa before dark and make successful landings there. Therefore, the 4th Wing departed on time and the 1st Wing departed three hours and thirty-eight minutes later, with the result that the two prongs of the attack were greatly separated in time and each would have to go it alone against whatever the Luftwaffe threw at it.

At 0935, the 4th Wing departed the U. K. at Lowestoft with 146 B-17s from seven groups flying in three combat wing formations. At 1000 it rendezvoused with its fighter escort of Spitfires and P-47s, and three minutes later it crossed in over the enemy coast west of Woensdrecht, Holland. At 1009 it turned south and seven minutes later took up a SE heading. At that point the 4th Wing was escorted by the 353rd FG (the Eighth's fourth fighter group which had gone operational five days before) and encountered a formation of FW 190s, the vanguard of some 300 single and twin engine fighters the Germans had ready for the bombers.

The 353rd's P-47s, however, could not engage the 190s for they had reached the limit of their range and were immediately forced to turn back. After doing so they providentially ran into twelve Me 109s and shot one down. It was one of only two kills by the penetration escort of P-47s, while RAF Spitfires claimed 8-1-0. Obviously the Luftwaffe knew what the escort would do. So the first gruppes, from Holland and Belgium, had waited, and when the escort turned back they let go at the 4th Wing, with 190s and 109s making coordinated attacks and coming in from every direction.

Over northern Belgium, from near Antwerp to the German border, 4 B-17s were shot down by 1033 when the Wing turned ESE. By the time course was altered again to almost due east at 1101, 3 more B-17s had gone down over Germany. Six of the first seven losses were from the 100th BG, which was flying the low position in the last combat wing. One of its lost planes managed to get to Switzerland where it made a forced landing.

From 1101 to 1131, Luftwaffe attacks of growing intensity battered away at the Fortresses, concentrating now on the lead combat wing, and 7 more B-17s went down. Then there was a lull in the attacks. At 1137 the bombers reached their IP and headed in on the bomb run, 127 B-17s bombing the Messerschmitt center at Regensburg at 1143 with 299.95 tons of bombs and scoring excellent results. At 1147 the formation turned south and underwent one last ferocious attack before it left a surprised Luftwaffe behind. But 3 more B-17s were lost, one of these making it to Switzerland, while 1 further B-17 turned off in the target area and tried to make it to Spain, but came down in France near Toulons.

At 1250 the battered formation was over the Alps. At 1333 it reached the Italian coast and headed across the Mediterranean over the Ligurian Sea. But 6 more damaged B-17s didn't make it — one crew bailed out over Italy and the others went down in the Mediterranean, with one of those crews being picked up and captured by a German seaplane.

The remaining 117 B-17s were off Sardinia by 1410, off Sicily by 1449 and reached North Africa at Bone at 1632. Thereafter some landed at their intended fields but many landed anywhere they could set down with dwindling fuel supplies.

While the 4th Wing headed across the Alps, the 1st Wing was finally off the ground and on its way, 230 B-17s from nine groups in four combat wing formations. They departed England at Clacton and Orfordness in two forces and met and joined up at the enemy coast SW of Woensdrecht, Holland at 1339. At the same time the P-47 escort joined the fully assembled 1st Wing as it proceeded inland.

Shortly afterward, when the escort turned back at its extreme range, the Luftwaffe (its planes thoroughly reserviced after the morning's fighting) struck even more furiously than earlier in the day. Over the border areas of Holland and Belgium the first wave of German fighters shot down 5 B-17s. At 1409 the 1st Wing altered course slightly over western Germany but kept on with a heading toward Regensburg. A second wave of German fighters smashed into the Fortresses and 10 more B-17s were knocked down by 1436. At that time the 1st Wing altered heading and made for Schweinfurt.

After a slight lull in the air battle, 2 more B-17s were shot down nearing the IP. The IP was reached at 1451 and from there to the target 4 more B-17s were shot down, and 1 other was lost at about this point or over the target. At 1457, 183 Fortresses began bombing their targets at Schweinfurt, dropping 304.8 tons of H.E. bombs and 130 tons of IB

bombs with telling effect. (Four other B-17s bombed targets of opportunity, while a single H2S equipped B-17 had bombed Frankfurt.)

Turning north off the target for a short distance, the 1st Wing lost 3 further B-17s. Then at 1508 it turned due west and headed back through the battle scarred skies it had just traversed. In the next hour, 3 more B-17s went down in Germany, as the Luftwaffe had once more refuelled its planes and begun sending them up again.

The full force of these final sorties was just about to be unleashed on the bombers when, at 1616, the first of 86 P-47s arrived to give withdrawal escort. In the lead was Col. Hub Zemke's 56th Fighter Group, and it tore into the German fighters with a vengeance near Eupen, Germany, claiming 17-1-3 single and twin engine fighters for the loss of 3 of its own planes and pilots. Still 2 more B-17s went down over eastern Belgium. Then the Spitfire withdrawal force arrived at 1641 and claimed 5-0-0, but yet 2 more B-17s went down over Belgium. At 1656 the battered 1st Wing made a final thirty degree turn to the right and headed straight for the Channel and England. But the toll of battle had still not ended — 2 final B-17s went down in Belgium and 2 more B-17s had to be ditched in the Channel before the remainder made it safely to landfall in at Felixstowe at 1731 hours — ending their four hour and eighteen minute ordeal by fire through the hell strewn skies of Europe.

In all, the 1st Wing had lost 36 bombers (ten from the leading 91st BG and eleven from the 381st BG flying the low position in the leading combat wing formation), while the 4th Wing had lost 24 (nine from the 100th BG and four from the 95th BG which together formed the last combat wing formation, and six more from the 390th BG flying the high position in the leading combat wing formation). The total loss for one mission was 60 bombers. Bomber gunners had claimed a record 148-20-62 (1st Wing) and 140-19-36 (4th Wing) enemy aircraft; P-47s had claimed 19-3-4; and Spitfires had claimed 13-1-0. Of the 174 1st Wing B-17s which returned to England — 3 had to be salvaged, 82 were severely damaged, and 37 others were damaged in one degree or another.

The Eighth had paid a bitter price, but it had hurt the enemy where it counted most. At Regensburg, every important building in the Messerschmitt complex was damaged and a number of newly finished Me 109s were destroyed on the field.

**Fortresses of the 96th Bomb Group at start of a mission from their base at Snetterton Heath. (Carl Moschel)**

At Schweinfurt, the bombers had scored 80 H.E. and 8 IB hits in the target area, 50 and 7 of these hits being on buildings. At the three ball bearing plants (Kugelfischer, VFK No. 1 and VFK No. 2) 97,013 sq. ft. of floor space was destroyed and 284,206 sq. ft. damaged. Of the vital machinery 2.5% was destroyed and 8.8% damaged, while 2.3% of finished stock was damaged.

In North Africa, after being made ready for further action, 85 Fortresses of the 4th Wing took off on 24 August to shuttle home to England, attacking Merignac airfield at Bordeaux on the way. Of these, 58 bombed and 3 were lost. The rest aborted or flew home without bombing. Of those which aborted and returned to North Africa, and the others which did not fly the shuttle mission, many flew home to England by skirting France and Spain and coming up the Atlantic coast of Europe over the Bay of Biscay. Others were left behind and sent to depots, their crews being ferried back to England by the Air Transport Command.

From 16 August through 9 September, the Eighth Air Force was involved fully, except for the great 17 August mission, in Operation STARKEY. It was a combined operation, with the Calais region as the focal point, to give Allied forces experience for a future cross-Channel invasion. Air forces concentrated on beating down the Luftwaffe and sealing off the region so a landing could be made. They attacked such targets as airfields, marshalling yards, beach defenses, gun emplacements and troop concentrations. At the climax, troops and vehicles were actually loaded into assault craft, and naval vessels were maneuvered to simulate a landing on the French coast in the Calais region.

STARKEY was executed in three phases. In the preliminary phase from 16 through 24 August, VIII BC and VIII FC operated on the 16th, 24th and one day between, flying 505 and 513 sorties and losing 13 heavies and 3 fighters while the fighters claimed 24-3-13. Mediums of VIII ASC flew 554 sorties in this phase. In the preparatory phase from 25 August through 7 September, VIII BC and VIII FC operated on the 27th, 31st, 2nd, 3rd, 6th and 7th, flying 1,001 and 975 sorties and losing 61 heavies and 6 fighters while the fighters claimed 10-1-3. The VIII ASC mediums flew 1,196 sorties in this phase. Finally, in the culmination phase, 8 and 9 September, VIII BC operated only on the mock D-Day, the 9th, and VIII FC on both days, flying 335 and 308 sorties and losing 2 planes each while the fighters claimed only 1-0-0. Mediums of VIII ASC flew 281 sorties.

As the operation unfolded, large scale air battles with the Luftwaffe did not materialize, weather impeded operations, and the Germans did not react as though they thought a landing was imminent. Thus the enemy did not cooperate with the rehearsal and only limited lessons were learned.

The Germans remained much more intent on keeping their fighters ready to prevent deep penetrations of the Fatherland. And it was due to this that the Eighth's heavies had one day of bad losses during the preparatory phase. On 6 September, 338 B-17s headed for aircraft and ball bearing plants in the Stuttgart area, while 69 B-24s flew a diversion. The Forts were forced by weather to attack targets of opportunity in Germany and France, and 262 managed to find something to bomb. But the Luftwaffe went to work that day and 45 B-17s failed to return. Some eighteen of the losses, however, were due to fuel shortages, occasioned by the bad weather, with twelve ditching in the Channel and their crews being picked up by Air Sea Rescue boats.

On 13 September 1943, a major change in the command structure of VIII Bomber Command took place. Thereafter, the 1st, 2nd and 4th Bomb Wings became the 1st, 2nd and 3rd Bomb Divisions respectively. Since February, March and May the former had had one or more Combat Bomb Wings (Provisional) under them to control two or three groups and facilitate operations employing the combat wing formation. On 13 September, these provisional units were integrated with officially designated Combat Bomb Wings — the first in each Division actually being the lineal descendant of the previous Bomb Wing (1st, 2nd and 4th), the others being new Combat Bomb Wing organizations from the U.S.

These changes in command structure are shown in the accompanying table. The resulting structure was employed for the rest of the war with the exception that in December 1944 the Bomb Divisions were redesignated Air Divisions.

Back in July, VIII Fighter Command had also instituted the employment of wings to control its groups. The 65th Fighter Wing went operational in July with the 4th, 56th and 78th Groups, then the 66th Fighter Wing took on the 78th, 352nd and 353rd Groups in August. Subsequently, the

EVOLVEMENT OF 8th AIR FORCE BOMBER COMMAND STRUCTURE, 1943

| FROM SPRING 1943: | | GROUPS | FROM 13 SEP 1943: | | GROUPS |
|---|---|---|---|---|---|
| 1st Bomb Wing | 101st CBW(P) | 91, 351, 381 | 1st Bomb Division | 1st CBW | 91, 351, 381 |
|  | 102nd CBW(P) | 92, 305, 306 |  | 40th CBW | 92, 305, 306 |
|  | 103rd CBW(P) | 303, 379, 384 |  | 41st CBW | 303, 379, 384 |
|  |  |  |  | 92nd CBW | 351 (401)** |
| 2nd Bomb Wing | 201st CBW(P) | 44, 93, 389 | 2nd Bomb Division | 2nd CBW | 389 (445) |
|  | 202nd CBW(P)* | 44, 392 |  | 14th CBW | 44, 392 |
|  |  |  |  | 20th CBW | 93 (446)(448) |
| 4th Bomb Wing | 401st CBW(P) | 94, 385 | 3rd Bomb Division | 4th CBW | 94, 385 (447) |
|  | 402nd CBW(P) | 95, 100, 390 |  | 13th CBW | 95, 100, 390 |
|  | 403rd CBW(P) | 96, 388 |  | 45th CBW | 96, 388 |

* The 202nd CBW(P) was active from 2 Sep 43.
** In Nov 43 the 351st BG was transferred to the 92nd CBW to which was assigned the newly arrived 401st BG; both of the groups were transferred to the 94th CBW on 15 Dec 43, and the 92nd CBW remained inactive until March 1944.

The B-17F Fortress flown by Major John B. Kidd and Captain E. E. Blakely at the end of its mission, 8 October 1943. (AAF)

67th Fighter Wing went operational in December 1943. By May 1944, each Wing would have five groups under it.

The B-26 groups of VIII Air Support Command continued operations through 8 October. Then all four groups were transferred to the Ninth Air Force which moved to England from North Africa on 16 October 1943.

On 16 September, the B-24s heard familiar words — they were needed in North Africa again. Consequently, the 44th, 93rd and 389th quickly moved off with 82 planes to furnish additional air support to the U.S. 5th Army, facing a grave situation at Salerno in Italy. By 19 September the three groups were in North Africa, and two days later they flew their first mission from Tunis. Two more followed on 24 September and 1 October (when the 109 factory at Wiener Neustadt was bombed effectively but at a cost of 10 B-24s). Thereafter, the Libs returned to England, starting on 3 October with the last one arriving home on 18 October. This ended their third and final journey to North Africa.

For the four week period following the close of STARKEY, the Eighth's heavies operated on seven days (twice on 23 September), and its fighters on eleven days. A total of 2,144 heavies were dispatched to targets, 1,638 bombed and 45 were lost on the eight missions. The fighters flew 2,428 P-47 sorties in the eleven days and claimed 53-16-12 enemy aircraft for the loss of only 7 Thunderbolts.

One mission was significant. On 27 September, four H2S equipped B-17s of the 482nd Bomb Group introduced pathfinder operations. Two flew in the lead position of each Fortress Division, so that when clouds covered the target at Emden they could use their H2S radar to aim and drop marker bombs — the following B-17s dropping their loads on the smoke trails of the marker bombs. In this way 178 B-17s, of 305 dispatched (plus the four pathfinders of which only two marked), bombed the port area with fair accuracy while 66 bombed targets of opportunity. Only 7 B-17s were lost. This was due in large measure to the P-47s giving escort over a German target for the first time — as they used 75 and 108 (4th FG) gallon pressurized belly tanks to extend their escort range up to 350 miles. The fighters, affording the Luftwaffe a shocking surprise by their deep penetration, claimed 21-2-6 for the loss of one P-47. Thus, on this day, the Eighth began to drive two more nails in the Nazi coffin.

From the earliest time of the Eighth in England there had been pressure for it to join the RAF in night heavy bomber raids. In September, to investigate how effective such mis-

sions could be, six missions were flown at night with RAF heavies. These were carried out by the 422nd BS of the 305th Group — to Boulogne on 8/9, to the Montlucon Dunlop tire factory on 15/16, to the Medane marshalling yards on 16/17, to Hannover on 22/23, to Mannheim on 23/24 and to Hannover on 27/28. A total of 30 Forts were dispatched and 28 completed their planned attacks. Two more missions were flown in October, and then the idea was shelved.

THE BLACK WEEK

Where the Eighth had lost 45 heavy bombers in the four weeks preceding the week of 8 through 14 October, the Black Week, in that seven day period it lost 148 heavies on four missions.

Industrial, port and city areas at Bremen were the main target on 8 October 1943, when the Eighth dispatched its largest mission to date, sending out 399 heavies. The mission also marked the first use of "Carpet" — airborne transmitters used to jam German gun laying radar — by forty Fortresses of the 3rd Division's 96th and 388th Bomb Groups. Enemy fighters concentrated their attacks on the lead wing of the 1st Division, with the low group, the 381st, losing 7 of its 18 B-17s; while flak and fighters did their worst to the third wing (13th Combat Bomb Wing) of the 3rd Division force, downing 10 B-17s of the 390th and 100th Bomb Groups. Total losses for the mission were 7.5 percent of the heavies dispatched.

The 100th Bomb Group led the 13th Combat Bomb Wing with the lead B-17 flown by Major John B. Kidd and Capt. E. E. Blakely. On the bomb run their Fortress was hit by flak but continued to the target and dropped its bombs accurately. Then it was bracketed by AA fire which destroyed the number four engine, damaged the control cables and shredded the left elevator. Instantly the plane went into a flat spin with its number four engine on fire and fell some three thousand feet before the two pilots managed to bring it back under control. As this occurred, the rest of the Group flew right through the heaviest concentration of flak and the deputy leader, two flight leaders and several other planes were shot down, and one plane was rammed by an enemy fighter.

Meantime, the lead plane was still flying. The fire in number four was put out as its cowl disintegrated and floated away in pieces, and the plane turned and headed back for England, following the most direct course out at 120 mph. But a lone plane over Germany was a dead duck which the Luftwaffe fighters always singled out, and in they came, mostly twin engine types. The gunners, some wounded and their

THE BLACK WEEK--OCTOBER 1943

| DATE | FORCE | TARGET | DIS | ATT | LOST | TONS | BOMBER CLAIMS | FIGHTER CLAIMS | GAF LOSSES* |
|---|---|---|---|---|---|---|---|---|---|
| 8 Oct | 1st Div | Bremen I/Area | 174 | 158 | 13 | | ) 167-22-85 | | ) 33/4/15 |
| | 2nd Div | Vegesack U/Y | 55 | 43 | 3 | | ) | | ) |
| | 3rd Div | Bremen P/Area | 170 | 156 | 14 | | ) | | ) |
| | VIII FC | | 274 | | 3 | | | 12-2-10 | ) |
| 9 Oct | 1st Div | Anklam I/Ac | 115 | 106 | 18 | 186 ) | ) 122-29-61 | | ) |
| | 3rd Div | Marienburg I/A | 100 | 96 | 2 | 218 ) | ) | | ) |
| | 2nd Div | Danzig P/A | 51 | 23 | 2 | 50 ) | ) | | ) 14/3/9 |
| | | Gdynia P/A | | 18 | 0 | ) 308 | ) | | ) |
| | 40th and | Gdynia P/A | 112 | 109 | 6 | ) | | | ) |
| | 45th CBW's | | | | | | | | ) |
| | VIII FC | | 140 | | 0 | | | None | ) |
| 10 Oct | 1st Div | Munster | 141 | 117 | 1 | 627 | 3-0-2 | | ) |
| | 3rd Div | Munster | 133 | 119 | 29 | | 180-21-49 | | ) 22/5/5 |
| | 2nd Div | Diversion | 39 | | 0 | | | | ) |
| | VIII FC | | 216 | | 1 | | | 21-1-4 | ) |
| 14 Oct | 1st Div | Schweinfurt I/BB | 149 | 101 | 45 | ) 483 | 186-27-89 | | ) |
| | 3rd Div | Schweinfurt I/BB | 142 | 128 | 15 | ) | | | ) 38/5/20 |
| | 2nd Div | Diversion | 29 | | 0 | | | | ) |
| | VIII FC | | 196 | | 2 | | | 13-1-5 | ) |

* GAF Losses = GAF Quartermaster report of aircraft lost
in combat / lost to other causes / damaged in combat.

interplane communications virtually gone, fought back for all they were worth — fought back so well that they shot down between seven and twelve of the attacking fighters and stayed in the air.

When the enemy fighters were at last left behind, the steadily descending Fortress approached the coast at 7,000 feet. As it did light flak opened up on the low flying plane and further riddled the bomber and knocked out the number three engine. Over the water and still settling, everything movable was thrown overboard to lighten the plane enough to get across the North Sea. It could not be ditched due to the injured crew members aboard.

The gravely damaged bird struggled on and finally made the English coast, flying low and with its fuel about gone. An empty airfield was sighted and Kidd and Blakely angled in for a crash landing. The gear was dropped, the plane touched down and instantly the brake cables gave away. The B-17 careened across the field out of control, the unwounded crew members aboard cradling and protecting the wounded, until it smashed into a tree at fifty miles an hour and stopped.

With over 700 holes in it, and structural damage from its crash with the tree, Fortress 393 had flown its last, but it had brought its crew back home. Four men were wounded, one fatally. The others would live to fight another day.

Of the twenty-one planes sent out by the 100th Group on on 8 October, seven failed to return, and one would never fly again. Among the pilots who returned safely from this mission was Lt. Robert "Rosie" Rosenthal, who had been on his first combat mission.

Next day, 9 October, four bomber forces were dispatched for the deepest raids yet into Germany. They crossed the North Sea and made landfall in over Denmark. The 1st Division force then proceeded southeast over the Baltic and at 1142 hours attacked the Arado factory, producer of major airframe components for FW 190s, at Anklam north of Berlin near the Baltic coast. Upwards of 200 German single and twin engine fighters of all types met this force with every trick they had, including rockets, air to air bombing and cannon fire from long range. The force suffered the highest loss of the day, but its bombs, dropped from 12,200 to 14,500 feet, hit every major unit of the plant.

Meanwhile, the other three forces continued east over Sweden and the Baltic and then attacked three targets in occupied Poland. The 3rd Division force made for Marienburg and, against light fighter and flak opposition, attacked the FW 190 assembly plant there at 1253 hours with superior accuracy and devastating results. Of 598 500-lb GP bombs dropped (68 tons of incendiaries were also dropped), 286 GP bombs scored hits in the factory area. Five buildings were totally destroyed, almost all the others were damaged, fifteen completed 190s were damaged or destroyed, and 114 workers were killed and 76 injured. When this force returned to England, being given withdrawal support by P-47s from the Leeuwarden area, it had covered 1,570 miles and suffered the loss of only two planes.

While the 3rd Division force hit Marienburg, the 2nd Division force made for Danzig while the fourth force, made up of B-17s from both the 1st and 3rd Divisions, headed for nearby Gdynia. Danzig was covered by a smoke screen from ships and floats in the harbor so that only 23 Liberators bombed the port area, at 1305 without effect. The other Liberators joined in the Fortress attack on the harbor area at Gdynia — where the cruisers *Nurnberg* and *Leipzig,* the *Gneisenau,* the *Lutzow* and *Emden* were berthed but hidden by a smoke screen. Although none of these naval vessels was hit, the bombing, from 1304 to 1341 hours, sank four other ships and damaged nine, including the liner *Stuttgart.*

This very deep penetration mission of 9 October had been a major success, but the cost in heavy bombers was relatively high. Total losses for the mission were 7.4 percent of heavies dispatched. More bombers had been lost in two days than in the preceding thirty, and the worst was yet to come.

On 10 October, the Eighth's heavies struck at Germany for the third day in a row. The briefed target, for the 1st and

3rd Divisions (the 2nd flying a diversion), was the built-up section of Munster, a rail center north of the Ruhr Valley; the intent was to disrupt the working population. As the 3rd Division led the way to Munster, followed by the 1st Division, the Luftwaffe scrambled nearly 300 fighters.

Once in the air the German fighters were guided by ground control, and for some time they were frustrated in preparing attacks. Again and again control informed them that the American bombers were under fighter escort and instructed them to take special care. Then came another call: "Achtung! Fifty bombers over Koesfeld, without fighter cover."

That was the 13th CBW, and immediately the Luftwaffe moved in on its prey. Twin engine fighters came into the area flying a 24-plane formation. Single engine fighters arrived in gruppes of 20 to 40 in echelon down formation. Attacks were then launched in overwhelming strength, concentrating on one group at a time from every clock position. The 190s and 109s pressed their attacks to 50-75 yards then took violent evasive action and came right back again. They flew through the leading elements to get at the low group until it was smashed, then concentrated on the high group and then the lead group. The 110s fired explosive cannon shells from guns slung under each wing at ranges between 200 and 1500 yards; Ju 88s attacked from 800 to 1000 yards, firing rockets from under each wing; and Do 215s and 217s flew parallel to the Fortresses some 1500 yards out and fired rockets.

Attacks on the 13th CBW began at the IP and continued against it, and other 3rd Division units, until P-47 escort arrived. In the 13th, the 95th BG was flying lead, the 390th high and the 100th low. There were thirteen B-17s in the 100th Group formation, one of them flown by Lt. Rosie Rosenthal on his third mission. He and his crew were the only members of the 100th to return from the mission — with two gunners wounded and two engines out. Two minutes after the concentrated attack on the 100th began the formation was well broken up and seven minutes later the entire Group was destroyed or dispersed, seven planes shot down before the target (one by flak) and five after the target.

The high 390th lost three planes before the target — one of these had its tail shot off by a rocket and crashed into another with both going down — and the lead 95th lost two planes with only six chutes seen from one of them. After the target the 390th lost five more planes, one when it was hit by a rocket and blew up near Gronau, and the 95th lost three more. One had its oxygen system set on fire just after bombing, one was lost at the rally point, and one blew up just before meeting fighter escort.

In the other 3rd Division wings, the 96th lost one Fort just after the IP, the 385th had one knocked down by flak on the bomb run and another lost later, and the 388th lost one B-17 just after bombing to hits by flak and fighters.

In all the 3rd Division lost 29 heavies while the following 1st Division was left almost completely alone and lost but one plane, mainly due to having fighter escort over the target. This escort and the withdrawal escort for the 3rd Division clearly saved many more bombers from going down.

Although the bombing at Munster was effective, it did not compensate for the high bomber losses which amounted to 10.9 percent of the aircraft dispatched. However, the number of enemy aircraft destroyed by the Fortresses and Thunderbolts did in some degree begin to balance the scales as the bomber gunners and fighter pilots further weakened the Luftwaffe, which in three days had lost at least 69 of its fighters to the Eighth Air Force.

After three days rest, the Eighth set out again on 14 October, its B-24s flying a diversion while the B-17s headed deep into Germany to a target visited once before — Schweinfurt. It had been tough the first time, it would be tougher this time.

The Forts crossed into Europe with the 1st Division leading and the 3rd Division following, escorted by 196 P-47s. Over Holland German single engine fighters appeared and concentrated on the Thunderbolts to limit their escort range and generally succeeded in their purpose. However, the 353rd Fighter Group turned in a superlative performance, giving deep escort to Duren, Germany. Its P-47s, in three separate engagements, downed five 109s and six 190s before they had to turn back. Two P-47s were lost as a result of the action.

As soon as the last Thunderbolts withdrew having reached the limit of their endurance, the bulk of some 400 enemy fighters began coming in on the bombers. At first there were waves of 190s and 109s then large numbers of twin engine fighters firing rockets. Most of their attacks were concentrated on the 1st Division. When the twins had exhausted their efforts, the Me 109s and FW 190s came in again.

Thus there was little respite for the 1st Division on the way to the target and its B-17s took a frightful beating. The 40th CBW had been in the lead originally, but due to troubles in forming up over England caused by weather, the mission came to be led by the 1st CBW with the 40th's 305th Group flying low in its wing formation, which was led by the 91st Group, with the 351st aid 381st Groups flying high. The 40th CBW placed itself to the immediate left of the 1st CBW with the 92nd Group leading and the 306th high.

As was becoming usual, it was the lead units which took the brunt of the attack, with the low group singled out first. Of the 97 Fortresses dispatched by the two leading wings, sixteen aborted for mechanical or other reasons, and 28 were shot down before reaching Schweinfurt — 12 from the low 305th which got but three bombers over the target, 10 from the high 306th which got only five bombers over the target, 5 from the 92nd, and 1 from the 351st. Oddly, the leading 91st, with but seven planes after four aborted, suffered no losses before Schweinfurt. The trailing 41st CBW lost only one B-17 (from the 303rd BG) before the target.

Meanwhile, the 3rd Division which had taken a more southerly route after entering Germany was not seriously challenged until nearing the target. Then it underwent ferocious but limited attacks which knocked down 3 B-17s before bombing, all from the 96th Group.

Bombs were dropped on the ball bearing factories between 1439 and 1457 hours through two to four tenths clouds from 21,000 to 24,000 feet, and the bombing was highly accurate. The heavies had taken a fearsome beating getting to Schweinfurt, and they did not let the opportunity pass to give as well as they received.

In all 483 tons of bombs were dropped with 143 H.E. and 37 IB hits in the target area, 88 and 20 on buildings. At the three ball bearing plants 350,920 sq. ft. of floor space was destroyed and 1,156,115 sq. ft. damaged. Of the vital machinery 3.5% was destroyed and 6.5% damaged, while 20% of finished stock was damaged.

The serious effect of this raid against the vital ball bearing industry subsequently shocked the Reich into naming a czar for bearings production and led directly to a wide dispersal of the industry. This, in turn, made the bearings industry far less vulnerable to attack in future, and in this sense the raid, which could not be immediately followed up, was counterproductive. For never again would the bearings industry be so vulnerable to strategic bombing.

But all of this was still in the future as the mauled force came off the target and headed back west to run the gauntlet of Luftwaffe defenses in order to reach England. Fortunately, the crews did not know that worsening weather over England would prevent the P-47 withdrawal escort from taking off to protect them as they came out over France.

The Fortresses had to go it alone to get home, and go it they did—at a cost. The 1st Division underwent fresh attacks from the Munich area by 190s and then more twin engine attacks. This time it was the 41st CBW which took it on the chin, the 379th and 384th Groups each losing six planes after the target; while the hapless 305th lost one of its three remaining Forts; and the 91st, 92nd and 381st each lost one. In all, the 1st Division lost 16 Fortresses on withdrawal.

The 3rd Division was steadily harassed after the target and jumped by refueled single engine fighters nearing the coast. It lost 12 Fortresses on withdrawal, four more from the 96th, six from the 94th and one each from the 95th and 390th. The 100th Bomb Group, which had been able to dispatch only eight B-17s for Schweinfurt, got all eight over the target *and* all eight returned safely to base.

Total loss for the day was 60 bombers, plus three from the 384th which crashed in England after their crews bailed out safely, one from the 92nd which crash landed in England and burned out, and one from the 303rd which crashed after its crew successfully bailed out over England. Twelve of the 196 other returning B-17s had suffered major damage while 121 had lesser damage.

Not counting the five B-17s which crashed in England, the total losses for the mission were 20.6 percent of the heavies dispatched.

The Eighth and Luftwaffe had been in a slugging match, and on 14 October the Luftwaffe had landed a deadly punch. But it was not a knockout. Instead the Eighth was able to regroup, continue operations and wait to deliver its own knockout punch in the coming year.

The Black Week was over, with the Eighth having dealt out some critical blows against Germany (especially at Marienburg and Schweinfurt) but at the cost of 143 B-17s and 5 B-24s. It was clear that more and longer range fighter escort was needed for the heavies if necessary and telling deep penetration daylight strategic attacks were still to be delivered and losses were to be kept to an acceptable level of 5 percent. However, before such escort became effective, winter itself would give the Eighth's bombers a respite.

WINTER OPERATIONS AND GROWTH

The majority of Eighth bomber operations in the three months following 14 October were flown in worsening weather using radar pathfinder techniques to deliver attacks. Such techniques allowed the bombers to operate on days when they would otherwise have been grounded and on days when the weather made it impossible for the Luftwaffe to mount vigorous interceptions.

Employing H2S, OBOE and H2X radar blind bombing devices (the latter, first used on 3 November, being an American version of H2S which was a considerable improvement of the British model), from 3 to 14 PFF planes led fourteen of the twenty-two bomber missions flown in the remainder of 1943. For the most part targets were port and industrial areas.

On these missions, the Eighth employed an ever increasing number of B-17G aircraft, the ultimate model of the Fortress, the first examples of which had begun to arrive in England in August 1943. This model featured a power operated chin turret, giving the Fortresses much better forward defenses against the Luftwaffe — just as new B-24G and H models with power nose turrets did for the Liberators.

Only one Eighth bomber mission was flown in the last half of October, by some 200 heavies on the 20th, but there were eleven missions in November, eight of them pathfinder affairs to targets in Germany usually by 300 to 500 bombers. Only 69 heavies were lost on those eight missions. In December there were ten heavy missions, six PFF-led to German targets, one without pathfinders to Emden, two to airfields in France and the first NOBALL mission. December losses were 162 bombers, 2.7 percent of those dispatched. Over 500 bombers were sent out on all but one of the December missions, and on the NOBALL mission to CROSSBOW targets in the Pas de Calais area on the 24th, 722 heavies were dispatched.

CROSSBOW targets were special construction sites (to serve mainly as launching and storage facilities) for a forthcoming attack against England by German secret weapons — rockets and flying bombs. By the end of December 83 construction sites, centered in the Pas de Calais area, had been discovered and photographed. Seventy were about half completed. On 24 December, VIII BC dropped 1,745 tons of bombs on 23 sites from 478 B-17s and 192 B-24s. The bombing on this occasion was done by squadrons using individual sightings.

Attacks against such facilities by Allied air units in the U. K. were of such vigor from late December well into the new year that most of the facilities (including massive concrete bunker installations) were knocked out. Consequently, Flying Bomb attacks against England did not commence until June 1944, using more numerous and temporary sites.

Beyond regular operations during October, November and December, the Eighth engaged in 34 night missions. Two of these, in October, were bombing missions with the RAF; two, in November, were special photographic and instrument testing missions; the other thirty were leaflet dropping missions. During the latter, 36,347,348 propaganda leaflets were dropped over Germany, France, Belgium and Holland.

On the growth side, from October 1943 into February 1944, four new Fortress groups and five new Liberator groups went operational with VIII Bomber Command.

Of even greater importance, in the same period six new fighter groups joined VIII Fighter Command, bringing its total of operational groups to twelve. The swift increase of the number of fighters on missions and their effectiveness can be seen at a glance in the accompanying table.

The first of the new groups to go operational was the 55th Fighter Group, which entered ops on 15 October with P-38s — the first Lightnings to fly for the Eighth in almost a year. With an escort range up to a maximum radius of 520 miles for the P-38H with two 150 gallon jettisonable fuel tanks (640 miles for the P-38J which began arriving two months later), the P-38s were an immediate answer to longer range fighters to escort the heavies. However, there were only two groups (the 20th FG went operational on 28 December) and the planes did suffer from mechanical troubles on high altitude

EXPANDING FIGHTER OPERATIONS--FALL 1943

| DATE | | CLAIMS | LOSS |
|---|---|---|---|
| 15 Oct | 34 P-47, 36 P-38 swept the Dutch Islands. | | 0 |
| 16 Oct | 132 P-47, 39 P-38 sent on fighter sweeps. | | 0 |
| 17 Oct | 28 P-47, 35 P-38 sent on fighter sweeps. | | 0 |
| 18 Oct | 296 P-47, 33 P-38 supported bombers. | 1-0-0 | 3 |
| 19 Oct | 37 P-38 sent on a fighter sweep. | | 0 |
| 20 Oct | 321 P-47, 39 P-38 supported heavies attacking Duren. | 6-1-7 | 0 |
| 22 Oct | 349 P-47, 42 P-38 supported Marauders. | | 2 |
| 24 Oct | 205 P-47, 48 P-38 supported Marauders. | 1-1-0 | 0 |
| 3 Nov | 333 P-47, 45 P-38 supported heavies bombing Wilhelmshaven. | 14-5-7 | 2 |
| 5 Nov | 336 P-47, 47 P-38 supported heavies bombing Gelsenkirchen and Munster. | 18-5-13 | 4 |
| 7 Nov | 283 P-47 supported B-17s in attacks on Duren & Wesel areas. | 1-0-0 | 6 |
| | 49 P-47, 54 P-38 supported Marauders. | | 2 |
| | 50 P-38 swept Ostend, Lille, Lens, Calais. | | 0 |
| 10 Nov | 208 P-47, 58 P-38 supported Marauders. | | 0 |
| 11 Nov | 342 P-47, 59 P-38 supported heavies bombing Munster. | 8-1-3 | 3 |
| 13 Nov | 345 P-47, 45 P-38 supported heavies bombing Bremen P/A. | 10-3-6 | 9 |
| 19 Nov | 288 P-47 supported heavies bombing Gelsenkirchen. | | 0 |
| 25 Nov | 276 P-47, 55 P-38 sent to bomb St. Omer airdromes and sweep Lille area. | 3-3-4 | 2 |
| 26 Nov | 353 P-47, 28 P-38 supported heavies bombing Bremen P/A. | 36-3-9 | 4 |
| 29 Nov | 314 P-47, 38 P-38 supported heavies bombing Bremen P/A. | 15-5-6 | 16 |
| 30 Nov | 327 P-47, 20 P-38 supported heavies bombing Solingen area. | 0-2-1 | 5 |
| 4 Dec | 140 P-47 sent out to give bomber support. | 3-0-0 | 0 |
| 5 Dec | 266 P-47, 34 P-38, 36 P-51 supported heavies in attacks on French airdromes. | | 1 |
| 11 Dec | 313 P-47, 31 P-38, 44 P-51 supported heavies at Emden. | 21-0-7 | 4 |
| 13 Dec | 322 P-47, 31 P-38, 41 P-51 supported heavies attacking Kiel and Hamburg. | 1-0-1 | 3 |
| | 36 P-47 (359th FG on first mission) swept Pas de Calais. | | 0 |

escort missions which adversely affected their contribution.

An even better answer to effective long range escort came from the Ninth Air Force when in December it received the 354th Fighter Group, equipped with P-51B Mustangs. These planes were a match for anything the Luftwaffe had, and they had a maximum escort range radius of 650 miles with two 75 gallon drop tanks. From the start they were used to escort the Eighth's heavies and turned in an excellent performance although not without teething problems, such as machine guns jamming and refusing to fire in combat.

The Eighth received its own first Mustang group on 1 February 1944 when the 357th Fighter Group was transferred to it from the Ninth (in exchange for the 358th FG with P-47s).

With more and better escort fighters and with more heavies, now able to bomb in poor as well as good weather, the Eighth steadily developed its power and carried out meaningful operations into the new year. It thus prepared itself to deliver its knockout punch against the Luftwaffe and the German aircraft industry in early 1944.

On 3 November, the Eighth flew its first over 500 bomber mission, as 555 heavies and 11 PFF aircraft were dispatched to Wilhelmshaven. Bombing through 10/10 cloud cover, 539 heavies dropped 1,450 tons, creating extensive damage to ship building works in the vicinity of the aiming point.

At Gelsenkirchen, 5 November, PFF bombing scattered bombs over the town. Two days later, at Wesel 53 Forts bombing by PFF scored no hits in the target area while at Duren 57 Forts bombed by PFF with poor results.

Norway had a surprise visit from the Eighth on 16 November. The main target was the molybdenum mine at Knaben, furnishing Germany with 85% of its annual new supply of this steel hardening metal. The attack was made by 130 1st Division B-17s, dropping 313 tons of H.E. bombs which destroyed 10 of 23 buildings and severely damaged two others, put the conveyor belt out of operation and stopped operations at the mine for a period of time. Concurrently, 147 B-17s from the 3rd Division and 29 B-24s bombed the power station at Rjukan. Five direct hits blasted the power plant. Only one B-17 was lost from each of the two forces.

On 18 November, 102 B-24s were dispatched to bomb the aircraft engine and fuselage repair depot at Kjeller airdrome, Oslo, Norway. Seventy-eight reached the target and bombed from 12,000 feet with very good results, creating heavy explosions and large fires amongst the facilities. Nine of the Liberators failed to return, however.

On 25 November, VIII FC P-47s began bombing the enemy. Supported by the 78th and 356th FG's, the 353rd and 56th bombed the airdromes at St. Omer, using two different techniques. A Liberator was employed as a sighting aircraft for 50 P-47s of the 56th, each carrying one 500-lb GP bomb. Flying level, they dropped from 24,000 feet, but the bombing was inaccurate and eight planes suffered minor flak damage. The 353rd sent out 52 P-47s, 16 carrying one 500-lb demolition bomb each. They approached their target at 15,000 feet and turned into a dive bombing attack, with bombs released between eight and ten thousand feet. The lead plane, flown by the Group C.O., Col. Loren McCollom, received a direct flak hit which exploded the main fuel tank, and McCollom bailed out to become a POW. In all 14 P-47s bombed, but only three bombs hit the airfield. Six planes sustained flak damage, but the Eighth's fighters had entered a new era, one of bombing operations by fighters. There would be many more such ops, and ground strafing attacks, before the war ended.

While two combat wings of 128 B-17s flew toward Paris and aborted because of clouds over the target on 26 November, seven combat wings of B-17s and two of B-24s attacked the Bremen port area. The PFF bombing, 1,205 tons from 427 planes, achieved some concentration of hits SE of the center of Bremen, while other bombs landed from two to five miles from the MPI. Over 100 enemy aircraft were encountered, including several FW 200s or Ju 290s which attempted air to air bombing from 3,500 feet above the heavies but without success. In support of the bombers, the 56th FG had a field day, claiming 23-3-9 for the loss of one P-47 and pilot. Most victories were twin engine Me 110s, with six pilots scoring doubles including Lt. Col. David Schilling with two 190s.

Among the 25 heavies failing to return from Bremen was "Barrel House Bessie" of the 384th BG, piloted by Major William F. Gilmore. What happened aboard Bessie that day was a stirring example of the bravery and devotion to duty

**A 392nd Bomb Group B-24H Liberator on its way to bomb submarine docks at Bremen on 29 November 1943. (AAF)**

and flying mates displayed by many Eighth airmen throughout the war.

Approaching the target, Bessie suffered failures in both outboard engines and immediately began to fall behind its formation. Bombs were jettisoned as the plane tried to regain the formation, but one fully armed bomb hung up in the racks. A moment later Bessie came under heavy fighter attack and initiated evasive action while T/Sgt. Maurice V. Henry entered the open bomb bay and despite intense cold released the hung bomb. Then he returned to his position in the top turret as the number three engine was hit.

"At this point," reads his subsequent citation for the Distinguished Service Cross, "T/Sgt. Henry destroyed one enemy and damaged another from his position in the top turret. Despite violent evasive action, the enemy fighter attacks increased in intensity and many damaging hits were made on

the aircraft. The oxygen system was shot out, the pilot's aileron control and both pilot and copilot's rudder control were destroyed, and the entire electrical system including instruments and turret control were made inoperative.

"An incendiary shell struck the left side of the cockpit, slightly wounding the pilot and setting the cockpit afire. T/Sgt. Henry extinguished the fire although ill and vomiting from the acrid smoke. The enemy fighters were evaded in the clouds, but the aircraft was losing altitude and due to the failure of the inter-communications system T/Sgt. Henry made repeated trips through the ship to carry out orders of the pilot and to supervise the jettisoning of equipment to lighten the load.

"Breaking out of the clouds at 6,000 feet directly over the city of Emden, the aircraft was immediately engaged and further damaged by heavy and accurate antiaircraft fire, but by strong evasive action, escaped to the sea. By this time, the number four engine was completely out and it was impossible to feather the propeller. Number three engine had been started again but was giving only spasmodic power. Shortly thereafter, both number one and number two engines cut out and T/Sgt. Henry quickly and with great presence of mind assembled the crew in the radio compartment and prepared them for ditching. The radio equipment had been destroyed and it was impossible to transmit an SOS.

"A small boat was seen in the sea and T/Sgt. Henry immediately produced a flare and Very pistol with which to signal it. With no power, the pilot landed in the general area of the surface vessel, the aircraft breaking in two just aft of the radio compartment. T/Sgt. Henry assisted the other members of the crew to leave the ship and was himself the last to abandon it, renouncing all regard for his own survival. He delayed his exit further by searching for and finding the emergency radio which he took with him into the icy water. Due to the battle damage to the life rafts, the heavy swell of the waves, and the shock of entering the extremely cold water, members of the crew could do nothing to assist each other. T/Sgt. Henry, still grasping the emergency radio which he considered vitally necessary to rescue, and despite the valiant struggle, was washed away and lost."

Ten minutes after Bessie went down, a rescue boat picked up seven members of the crew, one in the water and six in a dinghy, and returned them safely to England.

On 29 November, 360 Fortresses were dispatched to strike at the Bremen port area with over 350 fighters in support. At

**Lockheed P-38H Lightnings of the 55th Fighter Group at 91st Bomb Group's Bassingbourne base, 12 December 1943. (USAF)**

Thunderbolts of the 353rd Fighter Group, with Lt. Jack Terzian's "Marty" in the foreground. (Jack Terzian)

an early stage in the approach some 80 Me 109s bounced the P-38 target escort group in an attempt to force it to abandon its mission. As a consequence this group, the 55th, lost 7 P-38s, while claiming only 3 109s, and had to withdraw. Twin engine Luftwaffe fighters were held back to hit the bombers at the point of their deepest penetration when escorting fighters would be thinned out. However, losses were kept to 13 of the 154 heavies which managed to attack, after two wings were recalled due to weather, and bombing was poor and scattered. The Luftwaffe gambit had achieved only limited success.

Next day, a PFF mission was flown against the industrial area of Solingen, and weather conditions kept all but 79 of the 381 heavies dispatched from bombing, with poor results. Only a few enemy fighters were seen by the bombers on a day when just 3 heavies were lost. However, three enemy operated P-38s were met that day. One came through a bomber formation. It had no Allied markings, and when a P-47 pilot pulled alongside "the Nazi dove for the deck". Another enemy operated P-38 was probably shot down by an VIII FC pilot.

On 11 December, 523 of 583 heavies dispatched attacked the Emden industrial area, dropping 1,431 tons of bombs but with poor results. German fighter reaction was fierce. At 1255 Luftwaffe ground control advised its fighters that one Allied formation was without fighter escort. This was the 3rd Bomb Division. Most of the 17 heavies lost that day were from it as 109s and Me 410s came in from 12 o'clock high three to four abreast, fired rockets from 400 yards, then closed to 200 yards firing cannon and machine guns. The day's losses would have been heavier if the 56th Group had not torn into some 100 enemy fighters hitting the bombers. They claimed 17-0-6 (of the day's bag of 21-0-7 by the escort) for the loss of two planes and pilots who collided during a cross-over maneuver.

It was a three pronged assault against Bremen, Kiel and Hamburg on 13 December with 171, 355 and 111 heavies attacking with 12 pathfinders. The bombing at Bremen was

With Mustang escort above, a B-17G, 42-37772, of the 388th Bomb Group heads for the target. (AAF via Harry Miller)

**B-17F Fortresses of the 91st Bomb Group at 20,000 feet over France enroute to Tours, 5 January 1944. (USAF)**

poor, but at Kiel there was concentrated damage on town and dock areas. Only 5 bombers and 3 fighters were lost.

Munster was one of two German marshalling yards raided on 22 December by 199 heavies. Among them was B-24H 42-7638 of the 44th BG. It had three engines damaged by flak over the target, managed to turn for home but, above the clouds and sinking fast, had no chance of getting back. As soon as it was out of Germany the pilot gave the bail out signal and three gunners jumped. They descended through the clouds but luck was not with them. They came down in the Zuider Zee and all three were drowned — one body being found the same day, the last the following August.

Before more of the Liberator's crew could bail out the plane emerged from the clouds and the pilot saw he was over water and changed the bail out order to a ditching order. The seven aboard took their ditching stations and the wounded B-24 settled toward the water, only to have something go wrong at the last second. It crashed nose down straight into the water and stopped abruptly. The copilot, stunned from striking his head on impact, managed to release his belt and floated through the torn open cabin roof above him to the surface. There he freed a dinghy and clung to it until picked up unconscious by a German patrol boat twenty minutes later. Subsequently, he became a POW and at war's end was returned to duty, the only member of the B-24's crew known to have survived. Four men had been reported dead, the three who bailed out and one killed in the crash whose body later floated to the surface and was found, and the other five were listed as missing in action.

Wreckage of the B-24 remained in the Zuider Zee (now called IJsselmeer), 16 miles ENE of Amsterdam, until 1975 at which time a team of the Royal Netherlands Air Force, in cooperation with the Department of Waterways and Army Engineers, excavated it and pulled it out of the water. In doing so they found the remains of the five missing men — the pilot still in his seat where he'd died instantly. The remains of four of the men, along with the ashes of the fifth whose remains had been cremated, were returned to their families in the U.S. for burial in their own land. For them it had taken 32 years to write finis to a mission.

On the last mission of 1943, 464 heavies bombed nine Luftwaffe airdromes in France on 31 December, losing 25

and claiming 26-14-28. Over 540 fighters escorted, losing 3 planes and claiming 7-2-1. One of the lost fighters was a P-38 flown by Lt. Harold Bauer of the 55th Fighter Group.

Returning from southern France after having been engaged in combat, he was low on gas and "Maydayed" fifteen miles off Lizard's Point at 14,000 feet. He was about to bail out when he saw an ASR launch. Bauer circled it and then ditched his Lightning as close as possible to the launch. The plane sank very quickly, but Bauer had time to climb out onto the wing, release his parachute harness and enter the water, being kept afloat by his Mae West jacket despite his heavy flying clothes. He had trouble extracating his dinghy and had just succeeded in getting it to float when the launch picked him up, five minutes after he'd entered the water. The incident had been the first case of a P-38 having been ditched and the pilot living to tell about it.

On its fourth mission of the new year, 11 January 1944, the Eighth sent out three task forces, totalling 663 heavies. The first, composed of five combat wings of the 1st Division, was to break into two parts over Germany and attack the aircraft assembly complex at Oschersleben and the parts factory at Halberstadt. The second, four combat wings of the 3rd Division, was to attack two aircraft parts factories in Brunswick. And the third, three combat wings of the 2nd Division, was to attack two aircraft parts factories in Brunswick, one a joint target with the second task force.

Weather interferred, however, and became so bad that the 2nd and 3rd Divisions were recalled. The 2nd Division turned back, but one combat wing succeeded in bombing a target of opportunity, the rail center of Meppen, just inside the German border. The 3rd Division was so close to its targets that while many groups turned back several went on to bomb their primary, 47 B-17s dropping on the Me 110 parts factory at Waggum in Brunswick. Other B-17s hit industrial targets at Osnabruck on the way home.

Meanwhile, the 1st Division carried out its attacks against Oschersleben and Halberstadt, the FW 190 assembly plant at the former being heavily bombed by 139 Fortresses. For their perseverence, these 1st Div planes came under the full vengeance of the Luftwaffe which struck just after the target. A number of the single engine German fighters were using drop tanks to give them increased endurance, and as the P-51 deep escort began to depart they dropped them and came in for all they were worth. Violent attacks by these planes and twin engine fighters ripped several Fortress formations to pieces, the 303rd Group losing ten B-17s, the 351st seven, the whole Oschersleben force losing 34 Forrtresses.

The 401st Bomb Group led one of the three combat wings to Oschersleben. As the main escort departed after bombs away it, like the rest of the force, was hard hit by the Luftwaffe, losing four B-17s. The losses would have been higher, however, if it had not been for the remaining escort — one P-51B Mustang. As a swarm of forty German fighters came in on the 401st's wing, the lone P-51 dove right into the midst of them, and for the next twenty minutes gave one of the greatest exhibitions of sheer courage ever seen.

"It was a case of one lone American against what seemed to be the entire Luftwaffe," the leader of the 401st Group that day said later.

"The sight of him out there, all alone, surrounded by all those Jerries, trading punches right and left, is something I'll never forget," the 613th Squadron C.O. said later.

A tail gunner reported that he saw the single Mustang pilot knock out a "positive" six enemy planes.

Officially, the pilot of the lone Mustang, which was named "Ding Hao!", was credited with 3-1-1. Of the mission he said: "I scared some of the enemy away by 'stooging' up to them suddenly. Others I gave a 'squirt', which caused them to break away.

"On the first encounter, which turned into a melee, my flight lost me. I regained bomber altitude and then discovered that I was alone. I spent half an hour chasing and scaring away attacking enemy aircraft from 21,000 to 15,000 feet. I had five combat encounters during this time.

"For the first two encounters and combat all four guns fired. On the third I had two guns, and on the fourth and fifth encounter only one gun."

The pilot was Major James H. Howard, C.O. of one of the squadrons of the 354th FG, Ninth Air Force. For his actions that day he received the Congressional Medal of Honor.

When the day's action was over, fighters had claimed 28-13-24 (14 victories by the P-51s of the 354th Group, 12 by the P-47s of the 56th Group), and bombers had claimed 125-36-33. Of 289 B-17s dispatched, the 1st Division lost 42; of 234 B-17 dispatched the 3rd Division lost 16; and of 140 B-24s dispatched the 2nd Division lost 2. For the third time in its history the Eighth had lost 60 bombers in one day. Five fighters, none Mustangs, failed to return.

The 11th January attack on aircraft factories in Germany was the first since October's Black Week, and it presaged the knockout punch the Eighth was now ready to throw against the German aircraft industry and the Luftwaffe. This would be a series of blows delivered by two to three times as many heavies as had operated in October, and they would be covered by a much increased and more effective fighter escort.

## THE BIG WEEK AND BIG B

Since November 1943 a coordinated attack against the airframe and final assembly plants of the German aircraft industry producing single and twin engine fighter aircraft had been projected. Code named ARGUMENT it was to take the form of a series of joint attacks by the 8th AF, the 15th AF and the RAF. It required good weather to assure visual daylight bombing of the German factories, but such weather was hard to come by in winter. Consequently, ARGUMENT was continually delayed in the months after it was set to be carried out.

In mid-February wind and rain and snow swept down off the North Sea across the face of East Anglia. The Eighth's airfields sparkled and glistened under the snow and all operations ceased. Then the weather warmed and men cleared the runways. The storms still persisted for awhile over the Continent, but by the 19th of February, the heavy clouds began to break up over central Germany. Three to four days of clear skies, allowing the visual bombing necessary to assure accurate attacks of pinpoint effectiveness, were predicted. ARGUMENT was on.

On the night of 19/20 February, the RAF opened ARGUMENT, subsequently called the Big Week, with a heavy raid on Leipzig, an aircraft center. Weather interferred with the bomber stream and losses were heavy. Next day, the Eighth joined the action, sending out its largest mission to date as it dispatched 964 heavies and 835 escort fighters, aided by 2 squadrons of RAF Mustangs and 14 of Spitfires.

By this time, the Eighth's bomber groups had such a full complement of aircraft that most Combat Bomb Wings were able to put up two combat wing formations — an A and a B combat wing. Thereby the following combat wing forces were sent out by the three divisions: 1st Division — 1A, 40A, 40B, 41A and 94 CW's to Leipzig; 41B CW to Bernburg; 1B CW to Aschersleben. 2nd Division — 2 CW to Brunswick; 14 CW to Halberstadt; 20 CW to Gotha. 3rd Division — 4A, 4B and 45 B CW's to Tutow; 13A, 13B and 45A CW's to Posen and Kreising.

The 3rd Division was first away, heading north. It crossed in over Denmark, then moved across the Baltic and, north and east of Berlin, turned south. It was to attack the Arado and Focke Wulf factories at Tutow, Germany and Posen and Kreising, Poland. Clouds covered these targets, however, and while two wings bombed Tutow by PFF four wings turned back and hit secondary targets (the Marienehe Heinkel plant and a shipyard at Rostock with very good results) and scattered targets of opportunity.

Meanwhile, the 1st and 2nd Divisions were on their way over Holland into the heart of Germany. Targets for the 1st Div were the three Erla Me 109 factories at Leipzig, the Junkers assembly plant at Bernburg, and the Ju 88 component factory at Aschersleben. The main 1st Div force, led by the 401st BG, overcame adverse weather and fought its way through German fighter resistance (which was also hindered by the weather) to bomb the 109 factories at Leipzig with excellent results. The other two CW's of the 1st Div, with target area support by 55th FG P-38s, also hit their targets but with lesser results.

Behind the Forts, the 2nd Div Libertors made for two Me 110 factories in the Brunswick area, the Ju 88 component factory at Halberstadt, and the Me 110 assembly plant at Gotha — receiving target area support from 20th FG P-38s. At Gotha clouds covered the area and a PFF attacks was made with little result. Of the other two B-24 targets only Brunswick was hit, with poor effect, but a secondary target at Helmstedt was hit with good results and targets of opportunity were also bombed.

Weather had seriously interferred with a brilliantly planned mission, and although a total of 885 heavies bombed, only a quarter of that number hit their primaries with telling effect. On the plus side, only 13 B-17s, 8 B-24s and 4 fighters were lost against total claims of 126-40-66.

On 21 February, with the 15th AF in Italy and the 9th AF in England grounded by weather, the Eighth turned most of its attention to important Luftwaffe air parks and airfields. The 1st Div was assigned airfields in western Germany, the 2nd Div the large air park at Diepholz, and the 3rd Div two Me 110 component factories and an air park around Brunswick. Great belts of clouds, however, thwarted most attacks.

Part of the 3rd Div could do no better than drop by PFF on the Brunswick area, while one its wings hit at Hannover. The best the rest of the bombers could do was attack eighteen targets of opportunity in wing or group strength.

While the day's planned bombing thus came to naught, the weather which caused that result also kept down losses. Of 859 bombers and 679 fighters dispatched, just 12 Fortresses, 3 Liberators and 5 fighters were lost. Total claims were 51-19-32. During one fighter engagement, when Capt. J. W. Wilkinson of the 78th Fighter Group dove on an Me 109 and his P-47 was still 800 yards away, the German pilot opened his canopy and bailed out.

Next day, the 22nd, the treacherously unpredictable weather again interferred seriously with the Eighth's plan of attack. The 3rd Division, detailed for that toughest of targets, Schweinfurt, abandoned its mission during assembly, after several collisions occurred. And one combat wing of 1st Div B-17s, attempting to carry out a feint by hitting the Aalborg fighter base in Denmark, found its target obscured by clouds which made attack impossible.

The 2nd Div was once again headed for the Me 110 assembly plant at Gotha. Clouds, however, strung out the B-24s to such an extent they were recalled over Holland. Some units then bombed targets of opportunity at the Dutch-German border.

About half the 1st Div's main force, five combat wings sent to attack two assembly plants and two component factories, got through to their primary or secondary targets. Oschersleben (FW 190 assembly plant) was passed up due to solid cloud cover, Halberstadt was hit with little result through clouds, Bernburg was hit with fair to good results, and Aschersleben was bombed with good results. Little damage was caused by attacks on other targets. In accomplishing these results the five combat wings of the 1st Div had had to meet violent attacks by single and twin engine Luftwaffe fighters, which cost them 38 bombers of the 41 missing for the day. But their escort really made the Germans pay, claiming nearly sixty enemy fighters shot down.

After three days, the Eighth's all out efforts of the Big Week were attaining only moderate success, thanks to the weather. And when that weather stayed bad on the 23rd of February, the Eighth took the opportunity to stand down from operations and give its exhausted bomber crews and even more worn down fighter pilots a day to renew their strength. Only the 15th AF, striking at Steyr, kept the Big Week offensive going on 23 February.

On 24 February, the Eighth came back to the attack with another three pronged mission. Schweinfurt headed the list, to be hit this time by the 1st Division which had first visited the ball bearing factories there on 17 August 1943, while the 2nd Division once more tried for Gotha. The 3rd Division would, as on 20 February, head for Tutow, Posen and Kreising.

Flying up over the North Sea and then east over the Baltic, the 3rd Div, five combat wings strong, once more swung

| UNIT | TARGET | DIS | ATT | TONS | LOST | CLAIMS |
|---|---|---|---|---|---|---|
| **19/20 February** | | | | | | |
| RAF BC | Leipzig C/Ar | 823 | 730 | 2291 | 78 | |
| **20 February** | | | | | | |
| 1st Div | Leipzig | 278 | 239 | 641 ) | | |
| | Bernburg | 54 | 37 | 83 ) | | |
| | Aschersleben | 54 | 43 | 86 ) | | |
| | T/O's | | 21 | 23 ) | | |
| 2nd Div | Gotha | 103 | 88 | 216 ) | | |
| | Brunswick | 89 | 77 | 195 ) | | |
| | Halberstadt | 72 | 0 | ) | 21 | 65-33-29 |
| | Helmstadt | | 59 | 173 ) | | |
| | T/O's | | 23 | 62 ) | | |
| 3rd Div | Tutow ) | | 105 | 252 ) | | |
| | Posen ) 314 | | 0 | ) | | |
| | Kreising ) | | 0 | ) | | |
| | Rostock | | 101 | 224 ) | | |
| | T/O's | | 92 | 201 ) | | |
| VIII FC | ------------ | 835 | | | 4 | 61-7-37 |
| **20/21 February** | | | | | | |
| RAF BC | Stuttgart | 598 | 552 | 1990 | 9 | |
| **21 February** | | | | | | |
| 1st Div | German A/Fs ) | 615 | 0 | ) | | |
| 3rd Div | Brunswick ) | | 81 | 200 ) | | |
| | Hannover | | 1 Wg | --- ) | 15 | 18-14-14 |
| | 1st/3rd T/O's | | 417 ) | ) | | |
| 2nd Div | Diepholz | 244 | 0 ) | 1499 ) | | |
| | B-24 T/O's | | 142 ) | | | |
| VIII FC | ------------ | 679 | | | 5 | 33-5-18 |
| **22 February** | | | | | | |
| 1st Div | Aalborg ) | | 0 | ) | | |
| | Oschersleben ) | | 0 | ) | | |
| | Halberstadt ) 289 | | 18 | 50 ) | | |
| | Bernburg ) | | 45 | 110 ) 38 ) | | |
| | Aschersleben ) | | 34 | 77 ) ) | | 34-18-17 |
| | Magdeburg | | 25 | 72 ) ) | | |
| | T/O's | | 9 | 20 ) ) | | |
| 2nd Div | Gotha | 177 | 0 | ) | | |
| | T/O's | | 74 | 185 | 3 ) | |
| 3rd Div | Schweinfurt | 333 | Abandoned | | | |
| VIII FC | ------------ | 659 | | | 11 | 61-7-26 |
| **24 February** | | | | | | |
| 1st Div | Schweinfurt | 267 | 238 | 574 | 11 | 10-1-7 |
| 2nd Div | Gotha | 238 | 169 | 382 | 33 | 50-10-20 |
| | Eisenach | | 44 | 89 | | |
| 3rd Div | Tutow, etc. | 304 | 0 | | | |
| | Rostock | | 259 | 620 | 5 | 23-11-5 |
| | T/O's | | 36 | 64 | | |
| VIII FC | ------------ | 767 | | | 10 | 37-5-13 |
| **24/25 February** | | | | | | |
| RAF BC | Schweinfurt | 734 | 663 | 2152 | 33 | |
| **25 February** | | | | | | |
| 1st Div | Augsburg ) 268 | | 194 | 498 | 10 ) | |
| | Stuttgart ) | | 48 | 108 | 2 ) | |
| 2nd Div | Furth | 196 | 142 | 328 | 6 ) | 23-7-13 |
| | Nurnburg | | -- | -- | ) | |
| 3rd Div | Regensburg | 290 | 266 | 390 | 12 ) | |
| Various | Diversion | 45 | 0 | 0 | | |
| VIII FC | ------------ | 826 | | | 3 | 26-4-13 |
| **25/26 February** | | | | | | |
| RAF BC | Augsburg | 594 | 528 | 1726 | 21 | |

down north and east of Berlin toward its targets. But each of them was heavily hidden by clouds, and again the hapless B-17s (all of them this time) had to go for secondary targets at Rostock. They met light opposition and lost only 5 Fortresses, one of which landed in Sweden.

The German fighters concentrated their efforts over Germany, and violent air battles were fought at Gotha and, to a lesser extent, over Schweinfurt. At the latter, five combat wings bombed, with good results, losing 11 B-17s with 143 being damaged, and claiming 10-1-7 enemy aircraft.

Inbound to and over Gotha the three combat wings of the 2nd Division met the brunt of the German's interception. In a series of ferocious air battles with all types of Luftwaffe fighters, 33 Liberators were lost including 13 from the 445th and 6 from the 389th, which made up the lead wing, and 7 from the 392nd. Bombing accuracy at Gotha (after the 389th had dropped in error when its lead bombardier collapsed from lack of oxygen) was good to excellent. There was great destruction at the Me 110 assembly plant but unfortunately the key machine shops were virtually undamaged and less than a month's production would be lost. Also hit was the BMW engine plant at Eisenach, an opportunity target.

When all was over on the 24th, the Eighth had lost 49 heavies and 10 fighters while claiming 120-27-45, and two of its three forces had effectively damaged their primaries.

That night, the RAF laid on a strong attack against Schweinfurt but night area bombing was seldom effective against pin point targets. Of the 663 bombers which bombed, 511 Lancasters, 142 Halifaxes and 10 Mosquitos, only 22 were plotted over the ball bearing factories while bombs from 312 fell up to three miles from them.

On 25 February, the Big Week reached its climax as the Eighth undertook its fifth major attack in six days. While 45 heavies, mostly B-24s, flew a diversion: The 1st Div sent 268 B-17s against the Me 410 assembly plant at Augsburg and the VFK ball bearing works at Stuttgart. The 2nd Div sent 196 B-24s to the Me 110 component factory and finished aircraft park at Furth. The 3rd Div sent its Fortresses to Regensburg, which it had first visited on 17 August 1943, dispatching 110 to attack the Me 109 component factory at Prufening and 180 the Me 109 assembly plant at Obertraubling.

The 3rd Div arrived at Regensburg shortly after 111 B-17s and B-24s of the 15th AF had attacked and scored many hits on the Prufening factory. These planes had drawn over 200 enemy fighters in the course of their attack, losing 33 bombers while claiming, with their escort, some 90 of the enemy. Consequently the B-17s of the 3rd Div faced only some 50 German fighters, but still strong flak defenses, and they turned in bombing which was excellent to superb. After the day's ministrations by the 15th and 8th, Prufening was shattered and Obertraubling was heavily damaged.

Meanwhile, the 1st Div secured excellent and fair results with its bombing at Augsburg and Stuttgart, and the 2nd Div turned in a good performance at Furth, including damage to 38 of 54 planes seen on the ground. For the day, 30 heavies and but 3 fighters were lost against claims of 59-11-26.

On the night of 25/26 February, the RAF closed out the Big Week by raiding Augsburg.

Typically, it was bad weather on the 26th which ended the Big Week, giving the German aircraft industry and Luftwaffe a chance to begin licking their wounds. The Eighth had delivered its Sunday Punch with a rain of blows and believed it had the German fighter aircraft industry on the ropes. But in fact that industry had suffered only a stunning blow, having lost less than a month's production of the key Me 109, FW 190, Me 110 and Me 410 fighter types, a blow it could take and from which it would soon recover. The real loss had once again been in the air as the Eighth's attacks brought the Luftwaffe up to fight.

Since the early days of Eighth operations the Luftwaffe had consistently transferred more and more fighter units and planes from other fronts to defend the homeland from the Eighth's attacks, so that by the Big Week there were some 1,000 single and twin engine fighters defending Germany and the Occupied Countries, though less than 500 could operate on a given day. From early 1943 on, however, the units had suffered a constant attrition of planes and, most important, pilots in contesting Eighth raids. In the Big Week, the German home defenses lost a further 200 to 300 fighter planes to the Eighth's bomber gunners and fighter pilots, and they lost many irreplaceable pilots — a loss they could not afford.

The Eighth's knockout punch had not finished the fight in February, but the Luftwaffe was clearly staggered. This was well illustrated on 29 February when 226 Eighth heavies went out to raid Brunswick from above a solid undercast, escorted by 511 fighters. For the whole mission only one German plane was spotted and shot down—a Ju 52 transport!

After the Big Week, the Luftwaffe would never again give constant and deadly challenge to the Eighth, but when key German targets were attacked it would rise in great strength for one more attempt to stop what was now an unstoppable Eighth Air Force daylight precision bombing campaign. This was clearly shown in the early days of March when the Eighth turned its attention to the ultimate target, Germany's capital — Berlin. The first of those attacks were met ferociously, then the Luftwaffe defenders stayed on the ground.

The Eighth set out for Berlin for the first time on 3 March, but extremely adverse weather conditions forced the mission to be abandoned, only 79 heavies out of nearly 900 dispatched bombing targets of opportunity through 10/10 cloud. Escort was provided by 12 P-47 groups, 3 P-38 groups (the 364th flying its first mission) and 4 P-51 groups (two from the Ninth, the 357th and the 4th which had converted to Mustangs four days before).

In the course of the mission, the P-38s of the 55th FG continued on to Berlin, half of them reaching there to become the first AAF planes to fly over the German capital.

Next day, 4 March, the Eighth tried again for Berlin, sending out over 500 Fortresses with 18 fighter groups on escort.

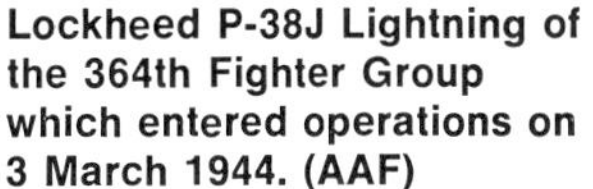

**Lockheed P-38J Lightning of the 364th Fighter Group which entered operations on 3 March 1944. (AAF)**

```
              THE EIGHTH'S FIRST BIG B ATTACKS, MARCH 1944

                                    ATTACKING
   DATE   BOMBER UNIT      DIS   PRI   T/Os   LOST   CLAIMS

   4th    1st Division     242    0    166 )         6-2-2
          3rd Division     260   31     33 )  15

     ESCORT:  563 P-47, 86 P-38, 121 P-51   23 Lost

     4th   2-1-0                 354th  1-0-0      2 P-51
           1-0-0grd   2 P-51    357th  2-1-1      1 P-51
     20th  None       3 P-38    359th  3-1-3      0
     55th  None       1 P-38    363rd  None      11 P-51
     56th  None       1 P-47
     78th  None       1 P-47    TOTAL  8-3-4 Air
     353rd None       1 P-47           1-0-0 Grd

   6th    1st Division     264 )        ( 18    41-24-45
          3rd Division     241 ) 413  61( 35    47-20-21
          2nd Division     226  196   2   16     5- 0 -0

     ESCORT:  615 P-47, 86 P-38, 102 P-51   11 Lost

     4th 15-0-1                355th  7-1-1      0
         0-0-10grd  4 P-51    356th  5-2-2      1 P-47
     20th 1-0-0      0         357th 20-1-7      0
     56th 10-2-5               359th  3-1-1      0
          1-0-2grd  1 P-47    361st  5-0-0      0
     78th 2-1-1      2 P-47    362nd  None       1 P-47
     353rd 3-0-0     0         364th  2-0-1      1 P-38
     354th 8-0-2     1 P-51    TOTAL 81-8-21 Air
                                     1-0-12 Grd

   8th    1st Division )                         )
          3rd Division ) 411  320    36   29 )  42-14-9
          2nd Division   209  150    33    9 )

     ESCORT:  612 P-47, 80 P-38, 184 P-51   17 Lost

     4th 16-4-5     1 P-51    356th  2-0-0
     55th  None     1 P-38           1-0-2grd   1 P-47
     56th 28-1-7              357th  7-0-3      1 P-51
          2-2-3grd  5 P-47   358th  None       1 P-47
     78th 0-1-0grd  0         359th  0-1-0      0
     352nd 2-0-0     0         361st  2-0-1      0
     353rd 5-0-3     1 P-47    362nd  None       1 P-47
     354th 1-0-1     0         363rd  5-0-0      1 P-51
     355th 2-0-0     1 P-51    364th  9-2-5      2 P-38
          5-1-2grd  1 P-47    TOTAL 79-8-25 Air
                                     8-4-7  Grd

   9th    1st Division )                         0-0-0
          3rd Division ) 418  331     0    6
          2nd Division   185  ---   54+    2     1-0-0

     ESCORT:  572 P-47, 88 P-38, 140 P-51    1 Lost

     No Claims.  1 P-38 364th FG lost.  54 B-24s
     of 2nd Div bombed their primary at Hannover
     while others bombed at Brunswick.
```

Again extremely adverse weather frustrated the mission. Over Germany a recall was received and the Forts turned back, some attacking Bonn, Dusseldorf, Cologne and Frankfurt with good results. One formation, however, "did not hear the recall" and kept on to Berlin. This was the 13th CBW, and 19 planes from the 95th Group and 12 from the "Bloody" 100th made it to Big B — the first AAF bombers over the German capital — and dropped 67 tons with unobserved results. The two groups claimed six enemy fighters and lost four and one bombers for the day. They were escorted over Berlin by P-51s of the 4th Fighter Group.

A total of 23 fighters were missing after the mission, the Eighth's highest day's loss of fighters to date, but most of them were victims of the weather. One P-38 of the 20th FG made it back to England after aborting with an engine out and being engaged by an enemy operated P-47. The pilot escaped the P-47 and subsequently landed in an abandoned English surface mine near an air base. His plane was wrecked in the landing and caught fire, and he had to have his shoe cut off before he could be rescued from the burning P-38, with only a sprained ankle and bruises.

On 6 March, the Eighth tried for Berlin once more, and this time made it, thus precipitating itself into one of the greatest air battles of the war. Leading the way were five combat wing formations of the 1st Div, their target the VFK ball bearing factory at Erkner, 16 miles SE of Berlin. Next came six combat wings of the 3rd Div, their target the Bosch electrical equipment factory in southwestern Berlin. Last came three combat wings of the 2nd Div, their target the Daimler Benz engine works at Genshagen, 20 miles south of Berlin. Escort was provided by 803 fighters.

The mission had to run the gamut of over 600 enemy fighter sorties, some German fighters making two sorties. The Luftwaffe's most intense thrust came against the 3rd Div, inbound roughly in three pairs of combat wings. Between Osnabruck and Hannover, the first and last pairs were attacked by 20 to 40 single engine fighters each, the Division's escort responding to these attacks. Then more than 100 Me 109s and FW 190s struck at the unprotected middle pair, the 13A and 13B Combat Wings. In forty-five minutes about 20 of their Forts were shot down, twelve from the 100th BG. After that came the intense flak of Berlin and, on withdrawal, another fighter attack. When it was all over the 3rd Div had lost 35 B-17s — including fifteen from the 100th and eight from the 95th, and seven from the 388th which were all lost on withdrawal to enemy aircraft.

Although the fighter escort had been unable to cover the 13A and B Combat Wings at a critical time, and another combat wing on withdrawal, it had otherwise done its job and taken a high toll of the Luftwaffe, especially of twin engine rocket carrying fighters in the target area. Yet even with generally effective escort the Eighth's Forts and Libs sustained their highest combat bomber loss of all time.

A total of 69 heavies failed to return on 6 March. Of that number 21 had fallen to enemy aircraft, 13 to flak, 4 to a combination of the two, 3 due to accidents and 28 to unknown causes (but mostly to enemy aircraft). Of the planes which returned, three were so damaged they had to be salvaged, 102 had major damage and 245 lesser damage.

Three groups of the 2nd Div had bombed their target effectively, while other Libs and the Forts had bombed in the greater Berlin area by pathfinder technique or had visually bombed targets of opportunity elsewhere. In all 1,507 tons were dropped on Berlin and 148 tons on targets of opportunity in other parts of Germany.

**North American P-51B Mustang of the 355th Fighter Group after crash landing in England on 16 March 1944. (AAF)**

A 390th Bomb Group B-17G, 42-39759, after it came down in France sometime early in 1944.
(Photo Jean Prieur)

After a day's layoff, the Eighth returned to Berlin on 8 March and dropped 928 tons on the Erkner ball bearing factory. Again the Luftwaffe rose in strength, but noticeably absent were twin engine types, probably due to the shellacking such types had taken on the 6th. The bombing put the VFK factory out of action for a considerable time. This plus substantial fighter and bomber claims of enemy aircraft, and with many less heavies lost, made 8 March a very successful day.

Following it up, the Eighth sent its Fortresses back to Berlin on 9 March, where they dropped 757 tons through 10/10 clouds, while the Liberators went to Hannover and Brunswick. Over Berlin, to everyone's surprise, no German fighters were encountered. For the day only twenty were seen, one of which was downed by a B-24. The 800 escorting fighters didn't even claim an enemy plane.

## FULL FIGHTER ESCORT

In general, up to March 1944, it had been the heavies alone which had won the upper hand in the air battles for Germany. They had forced the German fighter arm to engage and expand, withstood its blows and taken an ever mounting toll of its planes and pilots. Thereafter, the Forts and Libs continued to force the Luftwaffe to come up and fight on numerous occasions and to take their toll of its planes, but from the spring of 1944 on it was the long range fighter escort which took the heaviest toll. More and more the American fighters reduced the ranks of German fighters, in the air and also, after an escort, by going down to the deck and destroying them on the ground. The Eighth's fighters were now the hunters, and these were the days of the hunters.

From 26 March to 12 April, a special unit of P-47s known as "Bill's Buzz Boys" existed (named after Maj. Gen. William E. Kepner, C.O. of VIII FC). It was formed by 16 pilots from four groups led by the C.O. of the 353rd FG, Col. Glenn E. Duncan, whose brain child it was, and served to try out and develop techniques for strafing enemy airdromes. In eight missions "Bill's Buzz Boys" claimed 14-6-14 enemy planes on the ground, losing three P-47s and two pilots.

However, even as this unit evolved tactics, other groups were putting strafing into effect in a most telling way as Eighth bomber and fighter operations continued.

On 18 March, 511 B-17s and 227 B-24s with 927 escort fighters were sent to attack eight airdromes and aircraft component and assembly plants in the Friedrichshafen and Munich areas of south central Germany. Bombers claimed 45-10-17 and lost 43 — 19 fell to e/a, and at least 13 landed in Switzerland and were interned. Fighters claimed 37-4-7 in the air and 3-4 on the ground, losing 13.

Berlin was hit on 22 March, 750 heavies dropping 1,430 tons by PFF. Only 12 bombers were lost, plus 12 of the 817 escorting fighters (221 of which were from the 9th AF), the fighters claiming only 1-1 e/a on the ground.

On 27 March, 14 combat wings dropped 960 tons on GAF installations in France, concentrating on Bordeaux and the principal bases for long range German planes operating against Allied shipping in the Eastern Atlantic. Losses were 6 bombers and 10 of 960 escort fighters, fighter claims being 12-0-5 in the air, 24-1 on the ground and 2-0 on the water.

Nine days later 236 P-47s, 96 P-38s and 124 P-51s were sent out to strafe airfields in Germany and NE France. The

Two views of battle damage caused by flak to B-17G, 42-31968, of the 100th Bomb Group on 19 March 1944. (AAF)

355th FG shot up six airfields in the Munich area, claiming 8-1-2 in the air and 43-79 on the ground! The 4th FG hit five airfields in the Berlin area, claiming 2-0-0 in the air and 43-42 on the ground. The two groups destroyed mostly Ju 88s and Do 217s, and lost 3 and 4 P-51s respectively.

On 8 April, 644 heavies attacked aircraft factories at Brunswick and German airfields and control stations at Oldenburg, Diepholz, Quackenbruck and Rheine, and 34 were lost. Escort was provided by 712 fighters, which turned in a record performance at a cost of 22 fighters.

Next day, aircraft factories and repair depots at Warnemunde and Tutow on the Baltic and at Marienburg and Posen in Poland were targets for 542 heavies. Marienburg, extensively repaired since the great October raid, was well hit again, while Posen's FW 190 factory was seriously damaged by a force led by the 96th BG. Ten of 719 escort fighters, 18 B-17s and 13 B-24s were lost. Total claims were 65-15-30, the fighters getting 20-1-6 in the air, plus 15-5 on the ground and 4-3 on the water.

As escorted heavies hit Belgium and France on 10 April, the 20th and 55th Groups pioneered the high level bombing technique by fighters called Droop Snoot. The lead "Droop Snoot" P-38 had a transparent nose in which was a bombsight and a bombardier. When the bombardier sighted and released, the other bomb-carrying P-38s in the formation also let go their single 1000-lb bombs. The 55th dropped 14 tons on Coulommiers Airfield in the morning with fair results; the 20th dropped 13 tons on Gutersloh Airfield in the afternoon with good to excellent results. Now the Eighth's fighters were not only destroying the Luftwaffe in the air and by strafing, they were bombing it effectively as well.

On 11 April, 643 B-17s and 241 B-24s went out to hit at six FW 190 and Junkers component and assembly plants at Sorau, Oschersleben, Bernburg and Posen. The latter mission was thwarted by the weather. Elsewhere bombing was good but the defenses were deadly, and 64 heavies (9 B-17s of which landed in Sweden) were lost, about half going down to e/a. Bombers claimed 73-24-33, and the fighters again ran their claims over a hundred while losing 16.

Forts and Libs went out on 12 April, but their missions were abandoned because of weather. After the bombers turned for home, most of their 766 fighter escorts made sweeps and strafed, destroying 16 enemy aircraft in the air and on the ground while losing only 4. They also turned their attention to the railroads, destroying 10 locomotives. That was a harbinger of more trouble for the Nazis.

On 13 April, 600 heavies hit at Schweinfurt (where 1st Div lost 14) and twin engine fighter centers at Oberpfaffenhofen, Lechfeld and Augsburg, escorted by 871 8th and 9th AF fighters. In all 38 bombers and 9 fighters were lost, and again the fighters did well in the air and on the ground.

Weather prevented bomber operations on 15 April, but fourteen 8th and two 9th fighter groups went up to make low level sweeps over northern Germany, each within a specified area. Thirteen groups carried out their missions, destroying 58 e/a, 25 locomotives, 2 barges, 2 trucks, 2 power stations and 1 train. Losses were 33 fighters, 19 believed due to weather.

On 18 April, Berlin was the target for 745 heavies. Bomber losses were 19 with claims of 16-6-7. Claims by the 634 escort fighters were 4-0-1 and 16-12 with 5 lost.

On 24 April, 524 B-17s and 230 B-24s, escorted by 867 8th and 9th fighters, went after five Luftwaffe targets in the

| GROUP | AIR | GRD | GROUP | AIR | GRD |
|---|---|---|---|---|---|
| **8 Apr 44** | 370 P-47, 206 P-51, 136 P-38 | | | 22 Lost | |
| 4th | 32-0-10 | | 355th | 6-0-3 | 7-1 |
| 20th | 7-0-0 | 21-23 | 356th | 0-0-1 | |
| 55th | 1-0-0 | | 357th | 5-0-3 | |
| 56th | | 3-0 | 361st | 9-2-2 | |
| 78th | 7-0-2 | 0-9 | 362nd | 2-0-1 | 2-5 |
| 352nd | | 12-7 | 363rd | 7-0-4 | |
| 353rd | | 0-3 | | | |
| 354th | 20-1-16 | | TOTAL | 96-3-42 | 45-48 |
| **11 Apr 44** | 454 P-47, 241 P-51, 124 P-38 | | | 16 Lost | |
| 4th | 5-0-1 | 1-1 | 356th | | 13-3 |
| 56th | | 1-3 | 357th | 25-0-10 | |
| 78th | | 3-3 | 359th | 1-1-1 | 11-16 |
| 352nd | 3-0-0 | 20-19 | 363rd | 3-0-2 | 1-5 |
| 354th | 1-3-6 | 3-7 | 364th | 1-0-1 | |
| 355th | 10-0-13 | 13-4 | TOTAL | 49-4-34 | 66-61 |
| **13 Apr 44** | 504 P-47, 233 P-51, 134 P-38 | | | 9 Lost | |
| 4th | 5-0-0 | | 355th | 6-2-0 | 21-15 |
| 56th | 3-0-2 | | 356th | 2-0-0 | 2-2 |
| 78th | 2-1-0 | 1-1 | 357th | 7-1-0 | |
| 352nd | 1-0-0 | 10-3 | 363rd | 1-0-0 | 1-0 |
| 353rd | 0-2-0 | | 365th | 1-1-0 | |
| 354th | 14-1-8 | | TOTAL | 42-8-10 | 35-21 |

Munich area, and aircraft and tank component plants at Friedrichshafen. Twenty B-17s were lost to e/a, and total losses were 40 bombers, including 13 landing in Switzerland, and 17 fighters. Bomber claims were 37-21-23, and fighter claims were 66-6-20 air and 58-38 ground.

Sixty or more Eighth bombers were lost in one day for the next to last time on 29 April. Berlin was the target, and the 2nd Div met the only real air opposition, losing 27 Libs when fiercely attacked. Total losses, half to flak, were 63 heavies, plus 13 fighters. Claims totalled 87-28-45.

Berlin was attacked again on the 7th, 8th, 19th and 24th of May, the latter being the sixth mission to Big B within forty days.

On one of those missions, "Little Willie", a 388th BG Fortress, was over Berlin when a prop ran away on one engine and the supercharger went out on another as a result of flak hits. Immediately the plane fell behind its formation and was attacked by two fighters. While the tail gunner held them off the pilot nosed down at almost a mile a minute. When he finally pulled out he was all alone . . . fifty feet above the ground over Berlin. There was nothing to do then but head for home, following the "Autobahn route", and off went "Little Willie" across Germany on three engines.

It flew right down the main street of one Germany city and passed between two church steeples. A short while later it flew directly over a German army camp where Nazi soldiers paused in their calisthenics and gazed dumbfounded at the B-17. Then "Little Willie" went down the main street of another city on which a German girl was cycling. As the plane passed her the crew whistled and waved at the fraulein. Over Holland, the gunners shot off all their ammunition at German coast defense positions. On approaching one machine gun emplacement the crew saw a German soldier run to his post, slide in behind the gun and then think better of it and dive into a ditch as they roared over.

The North Sea was crossed just above the waves, then the touring Fort pulled up to 5,000 feet as it came in over the English coast and proceeded back to base.

On 12 May 1944, the vital German synthetic oil industry came under attack for the first time by the Eighth, as 886 heavies escorted by 410 P-51s, 265 P-38s and 201 P-47s hit refineries at Brux, and at Lutzkendorf, Bohlen, Leuna, Zeitz and Zwickau in the Leipzig area. Some 300 fighters opposed the bombers on penetration and over the targets, the bombers claiming 115 and the fighters 66-1-10 (plus 9-3 on the ground). Losses were 46 heavies and 10 fighters. The attacks were highly effective. At Bohlen the floods of oil loosed by the bombs killed and injured as many workers as did the bomb explosions. And at Leuna, where the Merseburg plant was the most important target of all, production was stopped and 14 days later had only risen to eight percent of normal.

Oil was the Achilles' heel of the German war effort, although this was not fully realized at the time by the Allies, and the German view of the attacks showed it. Reichsminister of War Production Speer later said, "The happenings of 12th of May had been a nightmare to us for over two years."

The Eighth again attacked the German oil industry on 28 May, hitting at Leuna, Zeitz and Lutzkendorf again and at the Ruhland and Magdeburg plants for the first time. Further crippling damage was done.

The immediate German reaction to the Eighth's attacks was to employ every means available to protect the critical oil industry in future — including decoy plants (the one at Leuna would be hit by as many bombs as the real plant itself), camouflage, smoke screens, balloons, blast walls and air raid shelters, plus deploying the strongest possible fighter forces and the heaviest concentration of AA guns to ward off attacks on the important plants. But there were no more Eighth raids for almost a month as in May and June the Eighth devoted a large proportion of its effort to tactical attacks in preparation for and support of Operation OVERLORD, the long awaited Allied invasion of France.

In mid-April, 25 French and Belgian marshalling yards were put in third priority for the Eighth Air Force — the GAF and CROSSBOW targets preceding them. The destruction of these yards was part of a joint effort by the Eighth, Ninth and RAF to disrupt transportation to such an extent that the Germans could not readily move reinforcements and supplies to the battle areas when the invasion began in Normandy.

On 1 May, 314 heavies dropped 1,007 tons of bombs on four French and two Belgian marshalling yards with fair to excellent results. Three bombers and three fighters were lost. Eight airfields and three marshalling yards in France and the Low Countries were hit by 772 heavies on 9 May. Two days later, three marshalling yards in Germany, three in France, two in Belgium and two in Luxembourg were struck by 669 heavies, dropping 1,944 tons. Losses were eight bombers and three fighters. During the last half of May, the Eighth made 38 attacks on marshalling yards and at least 21 on airfields. The heaviest was on 27 May when 1,067 heavies dropped 1,968 tons on one French and six German marshalling yards. The cost was nineteen bombers and seven fighters.

The fighters joined in the pre-invasion attacks with a "Chattanooga Choo-Choo" mission on 21 May. Under this plan Germany was divided into northern and southern parts, with an area in each part for each group — the P-51s having the areas furthest from base, the P-38s next and the P-47s the closest areas. On this day, 552 fighters were dispatched

**Liberators of the 389th Bomb Group, with natural metal finish B-24J in the foreground, heading out on a 1944 mission to a target in Europe. (AAF via Harry Miller)**

and 27 were lost for claims of: 91 locomotives destroyed of 225 attacked, 20-0-2 enemy planes in the air and 102-76 on the ground, plus many other ground targets destroyed.

With such bomber and fighter missions, the Eighth did its part in preparing for the invasion, but its greatest contribution to OVERLORD was the destruction of the Luftwaffe's planes and aircraft factories accomplished by its bombers and fighters. Because of that the once feared Luftwaffe would not be a factor of any importance as Allied troops stormed ashore on Normandy and established a bridgehead for further advances in June 1944.

From December 1943 to June 1944, the Eighth had also been engaged in one other campaign, attacks against CROSSBOW targets. In this period it flew 4,589 sorties against 96 ski sites (73 were severely damaged), dropping 7,968 tons of bombs; 2,045 sorties against rocket sites, dropping 7,624 tons of bombs; and 166 sorties against supply sites and dumps, dropping 479 tons of bombs. The Ninth and RAF also heavily attacked CROSSBOW targets throughout the period.

By early June, the Eighth had completed its growth and comprised a total strength of 40 bomb groups and 15 fighter groups. The 1st Bomb Division reached a strength of 12 B-17 groups in April, the 2nd Bomb Division 14 B-24 groups in May. The 3rd Bomb Division remained at a strength of 9 B-17 groups, but added 5 new B-24 groups in two Combat Bomb Wings during May and June. These five groups would continue with Liberators only for a few months, then convert to B-17s—three groups doing so in August, two in September.

Since March, three more VIII FC P-47 groups had converted to P-51s, and Fighter Command had received one new P-51 group (339th in April) and one new P-38 group (479th in May). Thus by June VIII FC totalled fifteen groups in three wings — seven with P-51s, four with P-47s and four with P-38s. Eventually all groups but the 56th (which retained P-47s) would convert to Mustangs.

Subsequently, the Bomb Divisions were redesignated the 1st, 2nd and 3rd Air Divisions in December 1944. In October 1944, the 67th, 65th and 66th Fighter Wings were placed under Division command from that of VIII FC.

D-DAY AND BEYOND

From 5 June through 8 June, more than 500 P-38s from the Eighth and Ninth Air Forces provided cover over the 6,483 vessels which transported assault troops across the Channel for the invasion of Europe. For twenty hours of each day, they prevented the intrusion of a single enemy aircraft.

On 6 June came D-Day, Operation NEPTUNE, the seaborne landings on Normandy which initiated the invasion, Operation OVERLORD. The Eighth's role on that great day began in the wee hours with the dispatch of 1,198 heavies against beach installation and 163 against Caen. There followed an effort to get 528 more heavies over the contested area, but clouds and the availability of only one PFF aircraft kept all but 37 from bombing. On a second mission, at 1330, 56 2nd Div Liberators bombed Caen. Then, 736 heavies, also on a second mission, were dispatched to attack transportation chokepoints in towns immediately south and east of the assault area, with 553 bombing.

Meanwhile, VIII FC put up 1,873 sorties in flying 107 missions on D-Day. In the course of these they destroyed 21 locomotives, 30 enemy aircraft and scored in a wide variety of attacks against trucks and goods wagons, armored vehicles, barges and tugboats, warehouses, radar towers, troops, artillery pieces and staff cars.

The day's total losses were 3 bombers and 26 fighters.

In support of OVERLORD, from 7 through 13 June, 4,478 Eighth bombers dropped 11,590 tons, and VIII FC flew 7,133 effective sorties. The fighters attacked six chokepoints and a road block on the 7th, and thereafter struck at rail and road bridges, rail junctions, airfields and coastal and other defense installations as the Normandy beachhead was secured. The cost of all these operations was 24 heavies (including four B-24s which were shot down on the 7th over their base by two Ju 88 intruders) and 109 fighters.

Although tactical targets were still of primary importance from 14 through 17 June, strategic operations were resumed on 14 June, and were again undertaken in earnest from 20 June as the battle of the hedgerows began in Normandy.

As these events transpired, the long feared and delayed German "Secret Weapons" attack on England began on the night of 12/13 June, when 23 V-1 Flying Bombs were launched and 4 made landfall. Three nights later the real assault began with 122 V-1s being launched and 44 landing in the London area. Thereafter, the city was under almost continuous fire until 3 September, when the launching sites in France were all captured. From 16 June to 30 August, 4,105 Eighth aircraft hit CROSSBOW targets, dropping 10,677 tons of bombs.

In the morning and evening of 20 June, 146 and 417 heavies went out to hit military installations in the Pas de Calais area. One B-24 was lost on each occasion. On the day's main mission: 512 B-17s hit eight oil targets in the Hamburg area; 358 B-24s escorted by six fighter groups went after the synthetic oil plant at Politz and an oil refinery at Ostermoor; and 341 B-17s and 19 B-24s with seven escorting fighter groups went against refineries at Magdeburg and factories at Fallersleben and Konigsburn. The first force lost 7 Forts to intense flak. 81 had major damage and 258 minor; the second lost 17 B-24s on penetration to vigorous attacks by 125

<pre>
        EIGHTH AIR FORCE SUPPORT OF NEPTUNE AND OVERLORD INVASION OF EUROPE
</pre>

| DATE | BOMBERS | | | FIGHTERS | | | |
| | ATTACKING | TONS | LOST | SORTIES | LOST | AIR CLAIMS | GRD CLAIMS |
|---|---|---|---|---|---|---|---|
| 6 June | 1729 | 4777 | 3 B-17/B-24 | 1873 | 26 | 26-0-8 | 4-9 |
| 7 June | 900 | 2419 | 1 B-17, 5 B-24 | 1445 | 27 | 31-1-13 | 24-4 |
| 8 June | 735 | 2012 | 1 B-17, 2 B-24 | 1469 | 24 | 31-2-5 | 21-11 |
| 9 June | None | | | 44 (on patrol) | | | |
| 10 June | 589 | 1398 | 1 B-24 | 1525 | 25 | 13-2-4 | 1-2 |
| 11 June | 640 | 1674 | 2 B-17, 1 B-24 | 921 | 9 | 5-2-5 | 0-1 |
| 12 June | 1278 | 3295 | 6 B-17, 3 B-24 | 988 | 20 | 25-0-10 | 2-0 |
| 13 June | 336 | 792 | 2 B-24 | 741 | 4 | 6-0-0 | 0-0 |

For D-Day, all Eighth fighters had black and white Invasion Stripes painted around wings and fuselage. When this obscured the aircraft letter on 352nd P-51s, it was repainted on fin and remained there. On 339th P-51B, at right, codes and letter were repainted over stripes. By September only the under-fuselage Invasion Stripes remained, as on Major Frederick H. LeFebre's YJ-L of 353rd FG, 44-14771, below.
(USAF and Ray E. Bowers)

Me 410s and 75 single engine fighters and lost 17 more and 3 P-51s later to flak and other causes; and the third met some 75 enemy fighters and lost 7 bombers and 3 fighters, but mainly to flak. Of the 50 bombers lost on the 20th, one B-17G, fourteen B-24H's and five B-24J's landed and were interned in Sweden. The day's claims were 12-3-8 by the bombers and 39-2-19 ground by the escort.

At Misburg south of Hamburg, where the Deurag-Nerag Refinery was in full production, 103 of the 497 tons dropped were on target and production was halted for forty days.

On 21 June, three forces totalling 868 B-17s and 368 B-24s were sent to Berlin and dropped 2,315 tons of bombs. Their escort of 961 fighters (520 8th AF, 441 9th AF) claimed 19-0-8 enemy planes air and 21-12 on the ground for the loss of 7 fighters. Intense flak and some air opposition caused the loss of 44 heavies, 14 of which (seven Fortresses and seven Liberators) came down in Sweden.

Concurrently, 144 B-17s and 70 P-51s (from the 4th FG and the 486th FS of the 352nd FG) were dispatched on the Eighth's first FRANTIC mission — an attack using Russian airfields as a terminus. Some 130 Forts effectively bombed the synthetic oil plant at Ruhland, south of Berlin, and proceeded east with 68 Mustangs. Over Poland about a dozen FW 190s intercepted the force and shot down 1 B-17 and 1 P-51, while the Mustangs claimed 6-0-3.

Reaching Russia, 66 Mustangs landed at Piryatin, 73 B-17s of the 45th CBW at Poltava and 66 B-17s of the 13th CBW at Mirgorod. Several planes landed at other points in Russia.

**Mosaic of Poltava airfield after Luftwaffe's attack on the night of 21 June 1944, showing many destroyed B-17s. (Impact)**

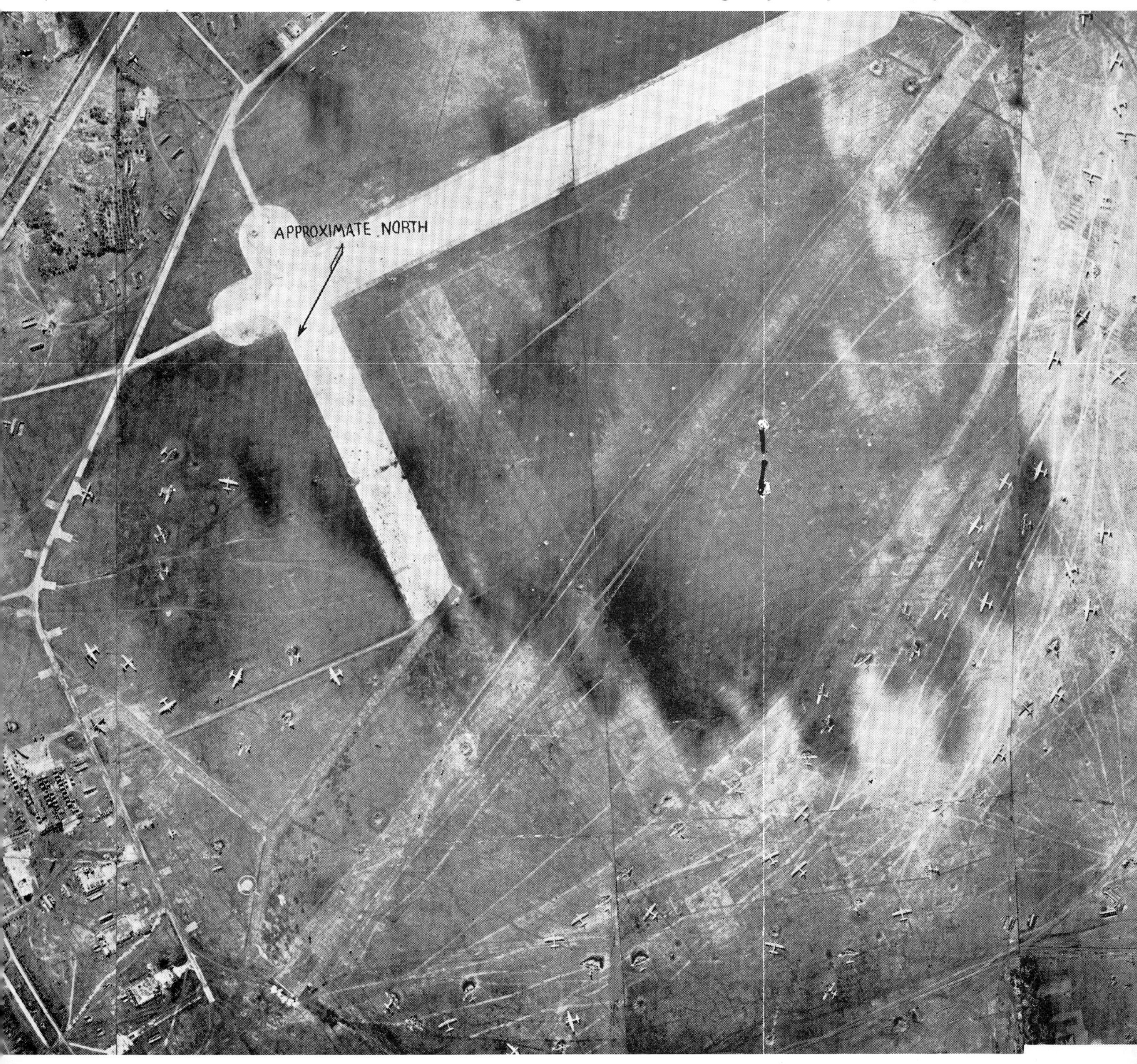

Unkown to all, an He 177 had trailed the bombers, and just after midnight some sixty Ju 88s and He 111s came in to attack Poltava. Two attacks, first bombing then strafing, were carried out in the next two hours. When they were over 47 B-17s were destroyed and almost all the rest damaged. Thus it was that the Eighth suffered its last high loss of bombers — losing 92 heavies and 45 crews in one day.

Less a few planes the remaining force, 71 B-17s and 55 Mustangs, departed Russia on 26 June, attacked an oil refinery at Drohobycz, Poland, and flew on to Italy. There some 40 B-17s joined in a 15th AF mission on 2 July, attacking the marshalling yard at Arad, Rumania, while the Mustangs also joined in that mission and others on 3 and 4 July — losing 6 Mustangs in all. Finally, on 6 July, the FRANTIC force headed home, nearly 70 bombers and 52 Mustangs, striking at the marshalling yard at Beziers, France on the way. Some bombers and fighters were left behind at various points due to wear and tear, their crews coming home by ATC.

From England on 30 June, while only 153 heavies were out hitting airfields in northern France and Belgium, 305 Eighth fighters scored fair to excellent bombing results against five Seine River bridges. In addition they turned in strafing claims of 50 flat cars, 20 locomotives, 10 trucks and 3 tank cars destroyed, and an oil storage depot, a canal lock and a power station damaged. The same day, Lt. J. Tucker of the Air Sea Rescue Squadron in a P-47 downed the first V-1 Buzz Bomb to fall to a member of VIII Fighter Command.

In June the Eighth's heavies dropped a record 58,595 tons of bombs in 22,581 sorties, operating on 28 days. Losses were only 230 bombers and claims but 45-21-61. Eighth fighters flew 25,150 sorties, operating on 28 days, lost 207 and claimed 284-12-101 air and 121-78 ground.

For the next two months, bombers and fighters each totaled some 37,000 sorties, operating on 50 and 55 days respectively, and flying an almost equal number of tactical and strategic missions. The heavies dropped 93,161 tons during the two months. Losses were 463 heavies and 318 fighters with air claims of 131 and 542 as the fighters continuously had more contact with enemy aircraft. Fighter ground claims in the period rose from 129-85 in July to 320-198 in August.

On many missions during the two months, more than 1,000 bombers and 600 fighters were dispatched from an average effective strength of some 1,750 heavies and 900 fighters.

In July the Eighth made large scale strategic attacks against oil, war industry and transportation targets in Germany on twelve days (from the 7th through the last day of the month). On the 4th, seven French airfields and four Loire bridges were tactical targets for 558 heavies. Attacks on the 7th against oil and aircraft factories by 1,129 heavies and 656 fighters cost 37 bombers and 6 fighters while putting 2,400 tons of bombs on targets. Munich was visited three days in a row, 11 through 13 July, with 55 bombers of the 3,122 dispatched on the three days being lost.

Lightnings of the 55th FG initiated a new dive bombing technique on the 14th when a Droop Snoot P-38, escorted by a standard P-38, dropped two gasoline bombs (loaded belly tanks with 2000-lb bomb fins attached) and a 200-lb incendiary on an ammunition dump in the Foret de Boulogne. As the planes departed, a fire was seen to be blowing.

On the 17th, the Eighth turned its full strength on 23 bridges, rail junctions and marshalling yards in northern France. Next day, 570 Libs dropped 1,425 tons on enemy troop concentrations in support of British and Canadian forces at Caen. Also on 18 July, the Eighth met the future when 434 Forts attacked the German experimental station at Peenemunde, a development center for secret weapons, including the V-2 rocket which in time showed man the way to the moon and the planets.

The hedgerow stalemate in Normandy was finally broken after an all out effort by Allied air forces against enemy positions in the St. Lo-Periers area, Operation COBRA, on the 24th and 25th. The Eighth sent out 1,586 heavies the first day, but weather kept all but 486 from bombing. Next day, 1,579 heavies went out and 1,508 dropped 3,395 tons of bombs with good results. Seven were lost mainly to flak. Following this, the U. S. First Army broke out of Normandy to the south, and then Gen. Patton's Third Army made swift advances across France to the east in the first half of August.

In August large scale strategic attacks against oil, war industry, ports and naval bases in Germany were made by the Eighth on the 4th, 5th, 6th, 14th, 16th, 24th, 25th and 30th. On 1 and 2 August, while U. S. forces in Normandy were on the rampage against disrupted German lines, over 900 heavies struck at French airfields and bridges on the 1st, and over a thousand hit at bridges, fuel dumps, airfields and Buzz Bomb launching sites in France the next day.

Berlin was raided for the thirteenth time on the 6th, along with oil targets at Hamburg and the FW 190 factory at Gdynia. Mustangs of the 55th FG provided target support at Gdynia then returned to England, a record setting escort flight of 1,595 miles out and back. The bombing there was done by 75 B-17s of the 95th and 390th Groups without loss on the Eighth's second FRANTIC mission. They went on with 66 P-51s of the 357th FG to land in Russia. From there, 55 Forts hit the Trzebinia, Poland oil refinery next day, and the following day 73 (escorted by 63 Mustangs) flew to Italy, striking at the Buzau and Zilistea airfields in Rumania on the way. The FRANTIC force then returned to England on 12 August, 69 Forts bombing an airfield at Toulouse, France as they went home. For the whole operation no bombers and but one fighter were lost. Only 7 enemy planes were shot down, all by the fighters — two on the 6th, three on the 7th and one on the 8th and 12th. Eight fighters and six bombers were left behind in Russia and Italy.

On 8 August, 497 B-17s aided Canadian troops, putting 1,488 tons of bombs on enemy troop concentrations and strongpoints south of Caen and losing 10 Forts to flak. Subsequently, the Canadians broke the stalemate below Caen, advanced on Falaise and with U. S. troops closed the Falaise Pocket, entrapping most of the German Seventh Army. On the 12th, heavies and fighter bombers helped isolate the Germans with extensive operations against all kinds of transportation, including horses and dog carts, east of the Seine.

On the 18th, the 56th FG made the first use of spike bombs as it flew dive bombing missions in the Amiens and Rouen areas. The C.O. of the 78th FG and one other pilot, taking their lead from RAF Typhoon squadrons, went out with six rocket projectiles under the wings of their P-47s. Six were aimed at a marshalling yard, two at a railroad control tower and three at stationary trucks—all missed! On the way home, Col. Fred Gray, with one rocket projectile remaining, aimed at the hulk of a small derelict ship off the beachhead and fired. "Well, that makes it 100%," he swore as he saw it apparently go astray. But then to his surprise the rocket, des-

```
           EIGHTH AIR FORCE VISUAL BOMBING ACCURACY*
              Within 1000 ft - Within 2000 ft
```

| PERIOD | 1st DIV | 2nd DIV | 3rd DIV | 8th AF |
|---|---|---|---|---|
| **1943:** | | | | |
| 1st Quarter | 18 - 36 | | | 18 - 36 |
| 2nd Quarter | 13 - 32 | | 11 - 29 | 12 - 30 |
| 3rd Quarter | 13 - 31 | | 19 - 48 | 16 - 38 |
| 4th Quarter | 25 - 46 | 32 - 58 | 27 - 47 | 27 - 48 |
| **1944:** | | | | |
| January | 34 - 61 | 23 - 48 | 41 - 60 | 35 - 58 |
| February | 42 - 76 | 26 - 49 | 46 - 77 | 39 - 69 |
| March | 31 - 64 | 20 - 36 | 39 - 70 | 31 - 58 |
| April | 34 - 62 | 21 - 43 | 32 - 58 | 29 - 55 |
| May | 44 - 68 | 34 - 64 | 33 - 62 | 37 - 65 |
| June | 49 - 81 | 32 - 62 | 35 - 65 | 40 - 71 |
| July | 42 - 73 | 26 - 56 | 44 - 77 | 37 - 69 |
| August | 54 - 84 | 36 - 65 | 42 - 72 | 45 - 75 |
| Sept/Oct | 29 - 61 | 32 - 56 | 46 - 72 | 38 - 65 |
| Nov/Dec | 24 - 54 | 24 - 44 | 25 - 47 | 25 - 48 |
| **1945:** | | | | |
| January | 29 - 59 | 34 - 61 | 24 - 56 | 29 - 59 |
| February | 50 - 80 | 57 - 81 | 40 - 69 | 49 - 77 |
| March | 40 - 76 | 45 - 73 | 30 - 58 | 38 - 69 |
| April | 64 - 91 | 58 - 79 | 52 - 80 | 59 - 85 |

```
    * Average percent of bombs dropped which fell
    within 1000 and 2000 feet of preassigned MPI's
    on visual missions under conditions of good to
    fair visibility.
```

cribing a beautiful parabolic arc, went nearer and nearer to the target and . . . wham! A perfect hit — the only one of the day. Later, rocket projectiles were used by other Eighth fighters.

Also on the 18th, the 479th FG, now under Col. Hub Zemke, former 56th FG C.O., turned in a most successful performance. Escorting B-24s which bombed Nancy-Essey airfield, the Group sent two squadrons down after bombing to strafe the airfield while one squadron continued with the bombers. The 32 strafing Lightnings made six to seven passes, resulting in claims of 60-53, most being twin engine types. Only one plane was lost when it was hit by flak, rolled over and crashed and exploded in the main street of Nancy.

Allied troops entered Paris on 25 August, and the Germans in France, fleeing almost everywhere, were clearly beaten. On 28 August, fourteen fighter groups flew separate fighter bomber or strafing missions to Holland, Belgium, eastern France and western Germany. They dropped 83 tons of bombs and turned in claims for 22 enemy aircraft, 189 loco-motives, 260 rail cars, 87 trucks, 21 staff cars, 3 tank cars and 5 barges destroyed. Losses were 19 fighters.

Eighth bombing accuracy, which had improved since the early days of operations but continued to vary, reached a new high in August — but would go still higher in 1945.

In September fourteen large scale attacks against oil, transportation and industry were made by the Eighth on twenty operational days. Cutting into the weight of these attacks were the Trucking Operations flown by its B-24s, to aid the armored elements of Patton's Third Army which had so far out-distanced their supply chain that their logistical position became critical. Between 3 and 30 September, 1,983 trucking sorties were flown by the Eighth to help out. In the first phase, 999 tons of supplies were flown to the Continent. In the second phase, from the 20th, gasoline had priority and nearly two and a half million gallons were flown to France. Only one B-24 was lost, going down to flak.

On 10 September, 1,340 heavies clobbered targets in the Rhine Valley behind the Siegfried Line and at Stuttgart, Ulm, Nurnberg and Wurzburg in southern Germany.

The Luftwaffe reappeared in strength next day as over 1,000 bombers and 600 fighters went to German targets. Some 400 enemy fighters rose to do battle, and once again the 100th Group felt their wrath. In all, 26 bombers were lost — twelve from the 100th and eight from the 92nd going down to two vicious fighter attacks. The escort protected the other bombers extremely well and for the loss of 30 fighters claimed 116-7-27, plus 34-39 on the ground. Top scoring fighter groups were the 55th (28 in the air), the 339th (15 air and 20 ground) and the 359th.

The 359th Fighter Group sent off forty-nine Mustangs at 0921 hours to provide penetration, target and withdrawal support. At 1115, in the vicinity of Gissen, Germany, fifty Me 109s and FW 190s were sighted at 32,000 feet preparing to attack the trailing bomber formation. Pilots of the 359th immediately dispersed them and drove them to the deck, destroying one and damaging two. At 1130, other 359th pilots dove down to jump enemy aircraft taking off from an airfield near Gotha, destroying five Me 109s in the air. Then they strafed through AA fire, destroying four Ju 88s and Me 410s and damaging four others. Shortly after this, escorting Mus-tangs of the Group spotted thirty 109s and 190s heading for the bombers at 30,000 feet. One element went after them, shooting down two and damaging another. Then at 1150 over one hundred German fighters were seen at 30,000 feet north of the heavies and the Group again went to the attack, destroying four, probably destroying two and damaging one, after which they downed four more in individual dog fights. Meanwhile, other pilots spotted and strafed a landing ground near Kelleda, destroying four and damaging nine parked air-craft. At 1205 near Eisleben after the heavies had bombed their target, fifteen 190s slashed at the bomber formation, and 359th pilots moved to the scene and shot down six of the enemy aircraft, probably downed two more and damaged another. Thereafter, following almost an hour of fighting, escort was terminated and the Group headed back for England. On the way home its planes destroyed seven locomotives to finish a great day.

**North American P-51D Mustangs of the 20th Fighter Group being prepared for a mission at their Kings Cliffe base in the fall of 1944. (Royal D. Frey)**

Fortresses of the 94th Bomb Group dropping their bombs on the marker bomb of the lead aircraft. (William T. Ashley)

September's big event, as Allied ground forces cleared most of France of the Germans and pushed through Belgium and even into Holland and Germany itself, was Operation MARKET. A landing in Holland by the First Allied Airborne Army to capture vital bridges over the Maas, the Waal and the Neder Rivers, it was designed to support the British 21 Army Group in a thrust into Germany across the lower Rhine. The effort, 17 to 26 September, almost succeeded and then failed, with British airborne troops at the forward point of Arnhem being decimated and the survivors having to withdraw while all other points were taken and consolidated.

On the 17th, 834 B-17s dropped 2,888 tons on 112 flak positions along the troop carrier routes, while Eighth fighters gave top cover to the routes and strafed ground defenses. In 538 sorties, 147 being bombing sorties, 12 fighters were lost and 49 battle damaged; claims totaled 8 enemy planes shot down (4th and 361st FG's) and 59 AA and gun positions destroyed plus 89 damaged. On the 18th, 246 B-24s dropped 782 tons of supplies from altitudes of 200 to 500 feet to the 82nd and 101st Airborne Divisions, with 7 Libs lost to flak, four more crash landing and seventy others damaged. Thereafter the Eighth continued to assist MARKET as it could, and on the 26th, 479th P-38s engaged more than forty enemy planes east of the airborne corridor, claiming 28-1-8 for the loss of but one Lightning to antiaircraft fire.

The Eighth resumed strategic attacks on the 20th and 21st and then from the 25th. On 27 September, the B-17s concentrated on oil and rail targets in Germany, while 315 B-24s hit at vehicle factories at Kassel. This force included 37 B-24s of the 445th Bomb Group, which wandered off course and bombed at Gottingen, some thirty miles from Kassel. Completely alone after bombing, they turned and headed for home. However, the German fighter controller had spotted the lone formation and called in one hundred FW 190s and Me 109s. They found the formation and came down out of the clouds and massacred the 445th. The sky ran red as in only five minutes the attackers shot down no less than 25 Liberators. Two more crash landed in France, two at Manston and one near its base at Tibenham. The Group had claimed 23 enemy fighters downed, but it had suffered the worst catastrophe ever to befall an Eighth Air Force group.

## CLIMAX, OIL AND JETS

In the summer of 1944 the Eighth was involved in two major struggles which continued into 1945. One began during the summer with the introduction into combat of German rocket and jet fighter aircraft, the other was the continuing campaign against oil begun in May.

At the heart of the German oil industry were the hydrogenation plants, turning coal into fuel and other derivatives, and producing half of Germany's oil products. Ten of the principle 18 hydrogenation plants alone turned out 80 percent of all German aviation gasoline. Oil was so critical to the German war machine that once Eighth bombing began 350,000 men worked day and night to keep the attacked oil plants going. Time and again they accomplished miracles, but from June on the Eighth kept hitting back everywhere.

The Merseburg GmbH at Leuna, near Leipzig, was the largest hydrogenation plant in Germany, producing synthetic fuels and lubricants, fixed nitrogen products and various organic chemicals. It was attacked eighteen times during 1944 by the Eighth. Almost every raid knocked it out of production for a time. When production resumed or before it did another raid was made. As a consequence, from the first Eighth raid in May to war's end (the RAF made three crippling night attacks in December 1944, January 1945 and April 1945), Merseburg's average daily production was only ten percent of normal.

| | HEAVIES | | TONS ON | EFFECT ON | |
|---|---|---|---|---|---|
| DATE | ATT | LOST | TARGET | PRODUCTION | RECOVERY |
| 12 May | 232 | 1 | 95 | 96% to 0% | 8% 14 days |
| 28 May | 59 | 0 | 41 | 8% to 0% | 22% 14 days |
| 7 Jul | 45 | 2 | 31 | 76% to 0% | 31% 7 days |
| 20 Jul | 148 | 2 | 87 | 53% to 0% | 35% 7 days |
| 28 Jul | 645 | 12 | 214 | 35% to 0% | |
| 29 Jul | 554 | 9 | 77 | 0% to 0% | 40% 60 days |
| 24 Aug | 191 | 11 | 75 | 0% to 0% | 25% 30 days |
| 11 Sep | 96 | 10 | 16 | 0% to 0% | No delay |
| 13 Sep | 133 | 6 | 83 | 0% to 0% | 4 wk delay |
| 28 Sep | 303 | 0 | 33 | 0% to 0% | 1 wk delay |
| 7 Oct | 114 | 2 | 1 | 0% to 0% | No delay |
| 2 Nov | 574 | 27 | 1 | 20% to 10% | Power loss |
| 8 Nov | 190 | 2 | 0 | 21% to 17% | Time loss |
| 21 Nov | 210 | 8 | 54 | 28% to 0% | 8% 14 days |
| 25 Nov | 672 | 7 | 55 | 0% to 0% | 1% 7 days |
| 30 Nov | 250 | 14 | 39 | 0% to 0% | 8% 7 days |
| 6 Dec | 472 | 4 | 46 | 8% to 0% | No report |
| 12 Dec | 348 | 2 | 18 | 0% to 0% | 10% 18 days |

EIGHTH BOMBING OF MERSEBURG REFINERY AT LEUNA

NOTE: Attacks of 12 May, 29 July and 30 Nov were PFF and Visual. Attacks of 28 May, 7 Jul, 20 Jul, 24 Aug & 13 Sep were Visual. All others were PFF.

Average bomb load carried by attacking planes was about 2.5 tons.

| | ENCOUNTERS | | COMBATS | | A/C LOSSES | | BOMBER | FIGHTER | FIGHTER |
| DATE | FTRS | BBS | FTRS | BBS | FTRS | BBS | CLAIMS | CLAIMS-AIR | CLAIMS-GRD |
|---|---|---|---|---|---|---|---|---|---|
| Jul 44 | 4 | 7 | 1 | 0 | 0 | 0 | 0-0-0 | 0-0-1 | 0-0 |
| Aug 44 | 21 | 30 | 10 | 7 | 3 | 1 | 0-0-1 | 2-0-1 | 0-2 |
| Sep 44 | 26 | 121 | 2 | 10 | 1 | 1 | 0-1-0 | 0-1-1 | 0-0 |
| Oct 44 | 42 | 61 | 27 | 5 | 0 | 0 | 1-1-1 | 6-0-1 | 1-0 |
| Nov 44 | 137 | 53 | 29 | 13 | 2 | 0 | 1-1-1 | 11-0-7 | 41-17 |
| Dec 44 | 74 | 43 | 15 | 8 | 1 | 0 | 0-0-0 | 2-0-6 | 5-9 |
| Jan 45 | 54 | 12 | 36 | 3 | 0 | 0 | 1-0-1 | 7-0-5 | 6-0 |
| Feb 45 | 118 | 45 | 71 | 39 | 1 | 2 | 0-0-3 | 20-1-17 | 1-8 |
| Mar 45 | 438 | 199 | 280 | 159 | 2 | 24 | 20-12-31 | 43-3-45 | 21-11 |
| Apr 45 | 319 | 169 | 234 | 148 | 0 | 24 | 36-31-19 | 56-5-67 | 46-18 |
| TOTALS | 1233 | 740 | 705 | 392 | 10 | 52 | 59-46-57 | 147-10-151 | 121-65 |

*EIGHTH AIR FORCE JET AND ROCKET COMBATS*

Other attacks by the Eighth (and by the Fifteenth from Italy) had similar effects on most German oil refineries and synthetic oil plants. The result of such bombing was the near ruination of an industry and the strangulation of the German military machine, through lack of fuels and loss of materials necessary for explosives and rubber production.

The oil campaign, while being one of the Eighth's greatest achievements, carried on concurrently with many other strategic and tactical operations, forced the Germans to use every possible means to try and halt it. Thus it was in defense of the most important oil target, Merseburg, that the Luftwaffe first employed the Messerschmitt Me 163 rocket powered interceptor.

Over Merseburg on 28 July, Eighth bomber formations were suddenly confronted by a startling sight — five white contrails at 32,000 feet, left by tailless rocket powered Me 163s racing through the sky at fantastic speed. Two came in at the bombers, and the P-51 escort turned into them but couldn't get near them. Next day the Me 163s appeared again over Merseburg, and this time Capt. Arthur J. Jeffrey, of the 479th in a P-38, dove and closed on one, scored hits and damaged it — the first claim against an enemy jet aircraft.

First major victories for the Me 163 came on 5 August when three Me 163s jumped as many Mustangs during a raid over Germany. In quick succession all three P-51s were shot down. But at the next meeting it was the Eighth that scored.

Cannon armed, rocket Me 163s were attacking B-17s near Leipzig on 16 August, and Lt. Col. John B. Murphy of the 359th had damaged one along with his wingman when he spotted another and closed on it. Again he scored hits and this time caused an explosion, destroying the Me 163 for the first jet victory of the war.

Along with the Me 163, the Germans were also bringing into action the first turbine jet fighter, the twin engined Me 262, also cannon armed and 100 mph faster than any Eighth fighter. On 28 August, Major Joseph Myers and Lt. M. O. Croy, Jr. of the 78th in P-47s jumped an Me 262 flying at 500 feet near Termonde, opened fire and sent it into the ground.

The first Me 262 fighter unit was formed in late September with thirty Me 262s. Under command of Major Walter Nowotny, a top German ace, and called the Kommando Nowotny, it did not lead a charmed life. On 6 October, Lt. C. W. Mueller of the 353rd shot down one of its 262s near Rheine while it was attempting to land. Next day, 7 October, Lt. Urban L. Drew of the 361st shot down two Me 262s after they took off from their base at Achmer. Col. Hubert Zemke and Lt. Norman Benolt of the 479th destroyed another near Nordhausen, and Major R. E. Conner of the 78th jumped yet another and shot it down. Meanwhile, near Leipzig, Me 163s were after the heavies and three pilots from the 364th destroyed one. That made it four Me 262s and one Me 163 in one day!

In November the Eighth's scourge of the jets continued. A 262 was nailed over Holland on the 1st, two more fell over Germany on the 6th, and on the 8th the Kommando Nowotny lost four Me 262s. One was apparently lost operationally, one fell to Lt. James W. Kenney of the 357th, another was shared by Capt. Ernest C. Fiebelkorn of the 20th and another pilot, and one was shot down by an unknown Mustang pilot. The last was the Me 262 of Nowotny himself. He was killed in the action and the battered Kommando was soon disbanded.

The Eighth employed an even more effective means of countering the jets on 18 November. It went after them at their airdromes while they were on the ground, and Mustangs of the 4th and 353rd destroyed 14 at Lechfeld Airfield.

Although the Eighth had the upper hand for the present, the jet menace remained. Action was more or less desultory in December and January, but the jets rose in greater strength in February and were extremely active in March and April of 1945. However, Eighth fighters, in full control of German skies, would more than meet the final challenge of the Me 262s in the last three months of the war.

In October and November, as winter weather came on, Eighth bombers operated on 18 days of each month, the fighters on 19 days. On 13 and 11 days respectively over one thousand bombers were sent out to oil, war industry, marshalling yard, airfield and (twice) tactical targets. Fighters escorted and continued attacks on ground targets afterward. On 14, 15 and 17 October nearly 3,400 heavies were sent to hit the transportation center of Cologne, dropping 10,000 tons of bombs. For the three days a total of fifty bombers and fifteen fighters were lost.

On 2 November the Eighth sent 1,100 bombers with 900 fighters to hit oil refineries and synthetic oil plants in Germany, precipitating "the biggest air battle of history". Over 400 German fighters intercepted several of the forces and when the battle was over the Eighth had claimed 183 in the air and lost 41 heavies and 28 fighters. The 352nd Group set a new record for air kills, and its 328th FS, led by Major George S. Preddy, set a new squadron record, getting 24 enemy planes in the air on one mission.

Operation MADISON came up on 9 November, an all out attack on the forts of Metz which were delaying Gen. Patton's Saar offensive. Under fighter escort, 1,120 Eighth heavies dropped 3,791 tons. Other fighters bombed and strafed rail targets in 200 sorties. Losses were 4 bombers and 4 fighters. Eleven days later the 5th Division entered Metz.

The Allies had penetrated the Siegfried Line in the fall but were held up by fortified towns in the Aachen sector. On 16 November, Operation QUEEN, a coordinated attack, was made on these points. With some fighters escorting, others strafing, 1,191 Eighth heavies dropped 3,873 tons of bombs. Losses were one P-51 to AA fire.

**On** 27 November, 510 escorted heavies bombed an oil storage depot and a marshalling yard in Germany. During that mission, the fighters encountered 747 enemy aircraft — the greatest number sighted in one day — and turned in a magnificent performance. For the loss of 13 they claimed 95 in the air and 3 on the ground and only one bomber was lost.

In December, the Eighth flew three large and seven smaller bombing missions in the first 16 days. Then on 16 December the German Army opened its last desperate offensive, The Battle of the Bulge. The Eighth aided the undermanned Allied ground forces as best it could on the 18th and 19th, but weather grounded it and other Allied planes for the next three critical days. The Wehrmacht took advantage of the situation and made considerable gains, but then the weather changed and air power put an end to the last German hopes.

As soon as the skies cleared the heavy bombers went out and strangled the enemy's efforts by bombing his supply and communication centers behind the salient. Such attacks were delivered by the Eighth every day from 23 through 31 December. In the first three days (with airfields also attacked on the 24th when a record 2,055 heavies were up and 4,302 tons were dropped) some 2,800 heavies attacked with over 40 bombers and 45 fighters lost against claims of 214 enemy aircraft.

On 24 December, 634 Libs went after fourteen communication centers and 1,421 Forts went out to hit eleven German airfields. Some intense fighting developed during the latter attacks. The lead group of one formation heading for Babenhausen airfield was jumped by 50 enemy aircraft south of Liege. The Fortresses and fighters claimed 18 of the GAF planes destroyed while losing 23 B-17s and 8 P-51s. Escorting another formation, the 359th FG fought with other enemy planes and claimed 13 destroyed and 13 damaged, but 8 B-17s and 4 P-51s of this force failed to return.

By the last day of the year, the heavies had done so well (and the breakthrough had been contained on the 27th) that part of the 1,262 heavies dispatched that day went out to hit at oil targets, a U-Boat yard and an Me 262 factory.

In January 1945, the Eighth struck at German communication targets behind the Western Front on eight of the first ten days (there were no missions on the 4th and 9th), averaging 1,000 sorties per active day. Thereafter, the Eighth returned to strategic missions while U. S. ground forces advanced to eliminate the Bulge, regaining the original battle line on 31 January.

For the last three weeks of January 1945 weather cancelled operations on nine days (including six of the last eight) and

| GROUP | AIR | GRD | GROUP | AIR | GRD |
|---|---|---|---|---|---|
| **2 November 1944** | | | | | |
| 4th | 4-0-0 | | 357th | 4-0-4 | |
| 20th | 28-1-6 | | 359th | 6-0-1 | |
| 55th | 18-1-2 | | 361st | 7-0-0 | |
| 339th | 1-0-0 | | 364th | 10-0-4 | |
| 352nd | 38-1-4 | | 479th | 1-0-1 | |
| 353rd | 3-2-2 | | | | |
| 355th | 7-0-1 | 23-0 | TOTAL | 127-5-25 | 23-0 |
| **27 November 1944** | | | | | |
| 56th | 3-0-0 | | 359th | 16-0-1 | |
| 352nd | 17-0-0 | | 361st | 5-1-0 | 3-0 |
| 353rd | 18-2-6 | | 479th | 2-0-1 | |
| 356th | 3-1-0 | | | | |
| 357th | 31-1-1 | | TOTAL | 95-5-9 | 3-0 |

**A 452nd Bomb Group Fortress is escorted by "Small Boy Here" a P-51D of the 78th Fighter Group. (AAF)**

Consolidated B-24M's of the 93rd Bomb Group drop supplies to Allied assault troops across the Rhine River. (AAF)

held them down to a minimum on three further days. On the other nine days, forces of 600 to 1,100 escorted heavies struck at marshalling yards and other rail targets, oil, industry (including a coking plant) and GAF control stations.

On 14 January, 360 Forts and 360 Liberators went after oil targets at Magdeburg, Stendal, Brunswick and Heide while 180 1st Div Forts struck at Rhine bridges at Cologne. Some 275 German fighters rose to give combat, but the best they could do was get 9 bombers of the 21 lost, and some of the 16 fighters lost. For their trouble, they paid heavily. Bombers claimed 31 enemy aircraft, fighters 161. The 357th FG led the way with an incredible performance, claiming 56½-0-4 (plus 1 on the ground) for the loss of only three Mustangs. The ½ victory was a 109 shared with a pilot of the 20th FG, which itself scored 19½-1-6.

Operations continued apace until 22 February when the Eighth participated in Operation CLARION, a massive blow against the German rail system by 8,000 Allied aircraft. The Eighth put put up 1,411 heavies which struck at 32 targets, 1,359 dropping 3,834 tons, and 822 fighters which escorted, strafed and included P-51 weather scouting forces operating in advance of the bombers. Losses were but 7 bombers and 13 fighters. Fighters claimed 7 enemy planes in the air, 22 on the ground, and destroyed or damaged over 100 locomotives. The next day, a similar operation was carried out.

These two days of operations were part of fourteen consecutive days, 19 February through 4 March, on which the Eighth operated more than 1,000 heavies and 500 fighters a day.

During operations to southern Germany on 25 February, the resurgent German jets took a beating. Eight Me 262s were shot down, seven of them by pilots of the 55th FG, and two pilots of the 364th FG downed the first Arado Ar 234 jet recon plane to fall to the Eighth Air Force.

Like a return to the early days, increased enemy U-Boat activity called for bombing attacks by the Eighth against sub-marine and shipbuilding yards at Kiel, Hamburg and Bremen on 11 March. Then on 14 March over 2,000 Eighth planes attacked important communication and industrial targets in western Germany. Similar attacks followed until Allied forces, which had moved across Germany in February/March to the Rhine securing a bridgehead over it at Remagen, crossed the Rhine in a great combined operation on 24 March 1945.

As part of the pre-crossing attacks, and in response to the increased tempo of operations by German jets, the Eighth began heavy raids against jet bases on 21 March. That day, eleven jet airfields were hit and one formation lost 4 bombers to 25 Me 262s, while fighters shot down 9 Me 262s for the day, six falling to 78th Group pilots.

On 24 March, as airborne landings led the way across the Rhine, 1,033 heavies bombed airfields in the morning losing 5, at midday 237 B-24s dropped supplies to airborne forces

| VIII FIGHTER COMMAND ON TWO BIG APRIL DAYS | | | | | |
|---|---|---|---|---|---|
| GROUP | AIR | GRD | GROUP | AIR | GRD |
| **10 April 1945** | | | | | |
| 4th | 1-0-0* | | 355th | 0-0-1* | 17-22 |
| 20th | 5-0-3* | 52-26 | 356th | 2-0-1* | |
| 55th | 2-0-2* | 27-8 | 357th | | 23-17 |
| 56th | 2-0-2* | 39-41 | 359th | 2-0-3* | 2-0 |
| 78th | | 25-22 | 364th | 1-0-0* | 11-11 |
| 339th | | 100-72 | | | |
| 352nd | 2-0-1* | | TOTAL | 20-0-13* | 297-219 |
| 353rd | 3-0-0* | 1-0 | | | |
| * All air claims were Me 262 fighters | | | | | |
| **16 April 1945** | | | | | |
| 4th | | 105-56 | 355th | | 69-45 |
| 20th | | 1-0 | 357th | | 2-2 |
| 55th | | 53-27 | 359th | | 5-3 |
| 56th | | 1-5 | 361st | | 13-4 |
| 78th | | 127-80 | 364th | 2-0-0 | 39-34 |
| 339th | | 116-39 | 479th | | 53-9 |
| 352nd | | 39-27 | | | |
| 353rd | | 109-43 | TOTAL | 2-0-0 | 732-374 |

across the Rhine losing 14, and in the afternoon 442 heavies bombed additional airfields. Covering these missions, Eighth fighters flew 1,294 sorties, losing 9 fighters and claiming 57 enemy planes destroyed in the air and 13 damaged.

With the Rhine crossed, Allied troops drove quickly into central Germany and the days of the Third Reich were clearly numbered. The Luftwaffe made one last major effort against Eighth heavies on 7 April, sending up 250 fighters (including 50 jets) as 1,300 Forts and Libs struck at an underground oil refinery, GAF control stations and munitions factories. Only 18 bombers were lost (two to jets and two to suicide ramming attacks), and for their trouble the enemy lost at least 85 fighters, 64 to Eighth fighters including five Me 262s.

The Luftwaffe had shot its wad, but it wasn't through taking it. Finished in the air except for limited interceptions, and with most of its pilots gone, it still had plenty of planes left. The Eighth fighters knew this, and they went all out against airfields to get rid of the remaining planes. On 10 April, strafing Eighth fighters destroyed 297 grounded enemy aircraft in a record performance — and when jets showed up they shot down 20 Me 262s in The Great Jet Massacre. Then, on 16 April, they turned around and destroyed over 700 enemy planes on the ground.

Further deprivations were inflicted in the following days even as the jets flew their last sorties against Eighth bombers on 19 April, losing six to the 357th and one to the 55th Fighter Group. Six days later, 25 April, Eighth bombers and their trusty fighter escorts flew their last missions against a crumbling Germany. The goal of 33 months of combat was reached on 8 May 1945, V-E Day, when Germany surrendered unconditionally to the Allies.

In operations over Europe from August 1942 to May 1945, the Eighth had proved the case for daylight strategic bombing, had met the Luftwaffe's best in a vicious series of air battles and beaten them, had gained control of the day skies over Europe making the invasion of Occupied Europe possible, had smashed the Luftwaffe completely in the air and on the ground, had crippled Germany's vital oil industry, had helped make a wreck of the German transportation system, and had affected in some degree almost every facet of Nazi Germany's aircraft, munitions, vehicle, tank and other war industries.

To accomplish this the Eighth had put forth an enormous effort and paid its price. That effort and the attendant losses are detailed in the accompanying table. The figures speak for themselves and the Eighth Air Force — the largest and most potent of all AAF Air Forces in World War II.

Additionally, strafing Eighth fighter pilots also took a heavy toll of ground targets other than enemy planes, including 4,660 locomotives destroyed and 2,791 damaged, 7,487 freight and oil cars destroyed and 25,317 damaged, and 4,882 military vehicles destroyed and 3,782 damaged.

Total Eighth casualties, as announced soon after Germany's surrender, were 43,742 airmen killed or missing and 1,923 others seriously wounded.

The performance of the Eighth Air Force would never be matched again in warfare, and no Air Force had done more to make a free world possible.

Unit markings applied to early Eighth fighters consisted of a squadron code and aircraft letter (which identified the plane within the squadron). The codes and their placement for the 1st, 14th, 31st and 52nd FG's are treated in the Twelfth Air Force Story. On 4th FG Spitfires, the squadron code was usually left of the national insignia and the aircraft letter to the right, in light grey.

When P-47s and P-51s in OD and grey finish went into use white recognition bands were painted on the nose, horizontally on the vertical tail and chordwise around both horizontal stabilizers and elevators. And chordwise white bands were painted around the wings of P-51s near the root. These recognition markings were in black on NMF planes. On OD and grey and NMF P-38s no recognition markings were applied as the type was easily identifiable.

All these Eighth fighters had squadron codes (white on OD aircraft, black on NMF planes) and aircraft letters. The codes were placed forward of the national insignia and the aircraft letter aft on P-47s and P-51s; the aircraft letter was on the outer coolant radiator housing of P-38s with the squadron code aft of it on the boom. After D-Day, Mustangs of the 352nd, 20th and 364th FG's had their aircraft letter painted on the tail.

From the end of 1943 and the spring of 1944, special unit markings began to appear on the fighters. The first of these were squadron symbols applied to the outer tails of P-38s in December 1943. Later (from March 1944) the aircraft letter was painted on the inner tails. Symbols and letter were white on OD P-38s, black on NMF P-38s.

From March/April 1944 group color markings were applied to the noses of P-47s and P-51s and to P-38s of two groups. Many nose markings were altered in style as time passed usually being extended to cover a greater area.

Black and white D-Day or Invasion Stripes were applied to all fighters in June 1944. They were removed from the upper surfaces in July, from the wings in September and disappeared entirely by the end of the year.

Squadron colored rudders were introduced by the 56th FG in March 1944, and in general were applied to all fighters from September to November 1944.

The basic application of special unit markings to aircraft of each Eighth fighter group is shown in the following pages of markings drawings, with the date when the specific marking was initiated. (The 358th FG, with the Eighth for only two months, is covered in the Ninth Air Force Story.) In a general sense, from mid-1944 on, Eighth fighters were in NMF, though some OD planes remained in service through the year. The one major exception was the 56th FG. It received P-47M's in January 1945 and subsequently gave them special paint finishes — matt black upper surfaces for the 61st FS, with red codes and aircraft letter; dark green and light grey shadow shading for the 62nd, with yellow codes and aircraft letter; dark blue and light blue shadow shading for the 63rd, with NMF codes and aircraft letter.

Recognition bands as applied to Eighth fighters: around tail surfaces and to nose on P-47s, above; none at all on P-38s, left; around tail surfaces, to nose and around the wings near the root on P-51s, white on OD aircraft, black on NMF aircraft. Planes are from 353rd, 20th and 4th Groups. (AAF, Royal D. Frey, Nitschke, Joseph Sills)

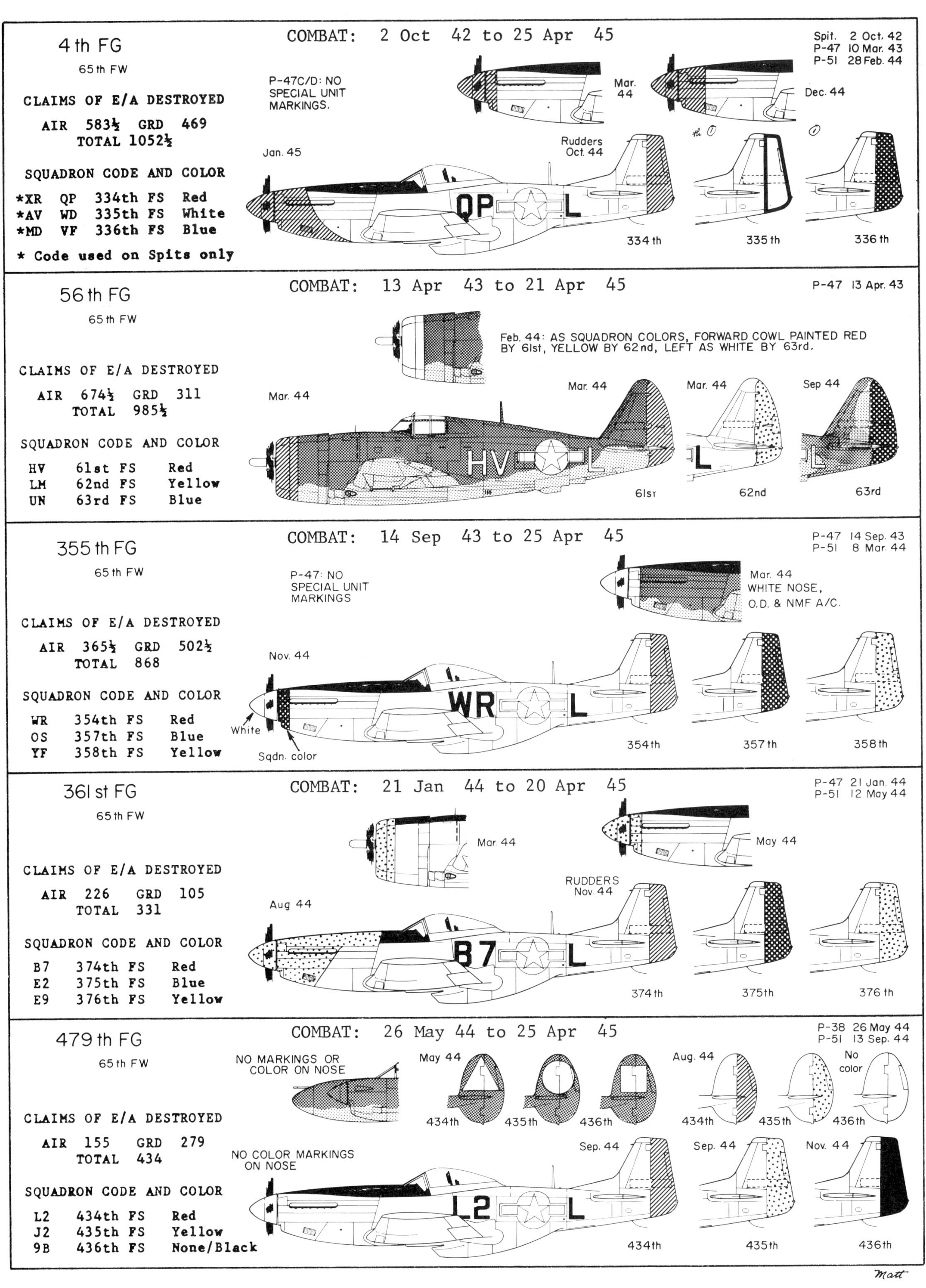

4th FG
65th FW
CLAIMS OF E/A DESTROYED
AIR 583½   GRD 469
TOTAL 1052½
SQUADRON CODE AND COLOR
*XR   QP   334th FS   Red
*AV   WD   335th FS   White
*MD   VF   336th FS   Blue
* Code used on Spits only
COMBAT:  2 Oct 42 to 25 Apr 45
Spit.  2 Oct. 42
P-47 10 Mar. 43
P-51 28 Feb. 44
P-47C/D: NO SPECIAL UNIT MARKINGS.
Mar. 44
Dec. 44
Jan. 45
Rudders Oct. 44
QP L
334th
335th
336th
56th FG
65th FW
CLAIMS OF E/A DESTROYED
AIR 674½   GRD 311
TOTAL 985½
SQUADRON CODE AND COLOR
HV   61st FS   Red
LM   62nd FS   Yellow
UN   63rd FS   Blue
COMBAT:  13 Apr 43 to 21 Apr 45
P-47 13 Apr. 43
Feb. 44: AS SQUADRON COLORS, FORWARD COWL PAINTED RED BY 61st, YELLOW BY 62nd, LEFT AS WHITE BY 63rd.
Mar. 44
Mar. 44
Mar. 44
Sep 44
HV L
61st
62nd
63rd
355th FG
65th FW
CLAIMS OF E/A DESTROYED
AIR 365½   GRD 502½
TOTAL 868
SQUADRON CODE AND COLOR
WR   354th FS   Red
OS   357th FS   Blue
YF   358th FS   Yellow
COMBAT:  14 Sep 43 to 25 Apr 45
P-47 14 Sep. 43
P-51 8 Mar. 44
P-47: NO SPECIAL UNIT MARKINGS
Mar. 44
WHITE NOSE, O.D. & NMF A/C.
Nov. 44
White
Sqdn. color
WR L
354th
357th
358th
361st FG
65th FW
CLAIMS OF E/A DESTROYED
AIR 226   GRD 105
TOTAL 331
SQUADRON CODE AND COLOR
B7   374th FS   Red
E2   375th FS   Blue
E9   376th FS   Yellow
COMBAT:  21 Jan 44 to 20 Apr 45
P-47 21 Jan. 44
P-51 12 May 44
Mar. 44
May 44
Aug 44
RUDDERS Nov. 44
B7 L
374th
375th
376th
479th FG
65th FW
CLAIMS OF E/A DESTROYED
AIR 155   GRD 279
TOTAL 434
SQUADRON CODE AND COLOR
L2   434th FS   Red
J2   435th FS   Yellow
9B   436th FS   None/Black
COMBAT:  26 May 44 to 25 Apr 45
P-38 26 May 44
P-51 13 Sep. 44
NO MARKINGS OR COLOR ON NOSE
May 44
434th    435th    436th
Aug. 44
434th    435th    436th
No color
NO COLOR MARKINGS ON NOSE
Sep. 44
Sep. 44
Nov. 44
L2 L
434th
435th
436th
Matt

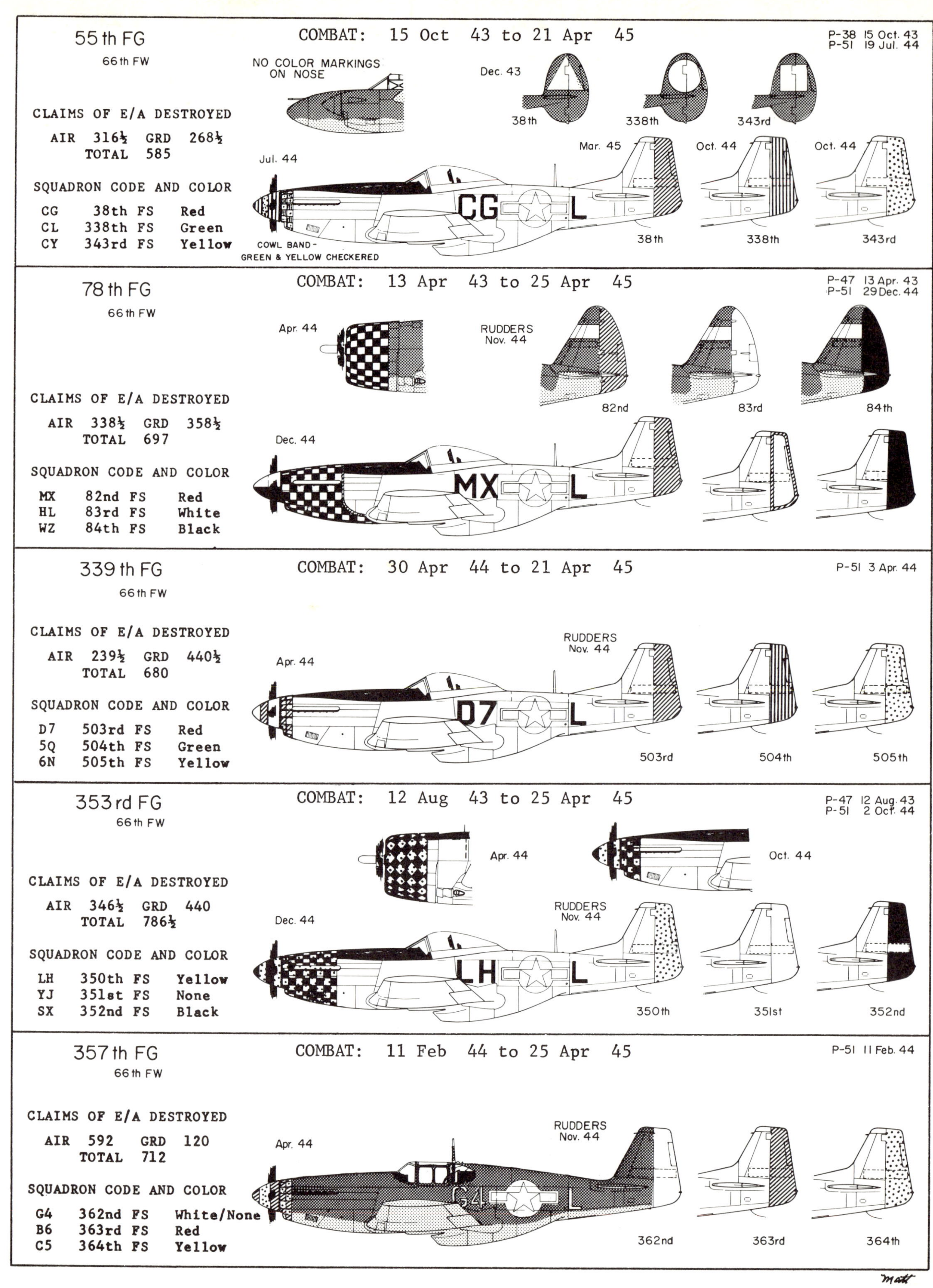

55th FG
66th FW
CLAIMS OF E/A DESTROYED
AIR 316½   GRD 268½
TOTAL 585
SQUADRON CODE AND COLOR
CG   38th FS   Red
CL   338th FS   Green
CY   343rd FS   Yellow
COMBAT: 15 Oct 43 to 21 Apr 45
P-38 15 Oct. 43
P-51 19 Jul. 44
NO COLOR MARKINGS ON NOSE
Dec. 43
38th
338th
343rd
Jul. 44
Mar. 45
Oct. 44
Oct. 44
CG   L
COWL BAND - GREEN & YELLOW CHECKERED
38th
338th
343rd

78th FG
66th FW
CLAIMS OF E/A DESTROYED
AIR 338½   GRD 358½
TOTAL 697
SQUADRON CODE AND COLOR
MX   82nd FS   Red
HL   83rd FS   White
WZ   84th FS   Black
COMBAT: 13 Apr 43 to 25 Apr 45
P-47 13 Apr. 43
P-51 29 Dec. 44
Apr. 44
RUDDERS Nov. 44
82nd
83rd
84th
Dec. 44
MX   L

339th FG
66th FW
CLAIMS OF E/A DESTROYED
AIR 239½   GRD 440½
TOTAL 680
SQUADRON CODE AND COLOR
D7   503rd FS   Red
5Q   504th FS   Green
6N   505th FS   Yellow
COMBAT: 30 Apr 44 to 21 Apr 45
P-51 3 Apr. 44
Apr. 44
RUDDERS Nov. 44
D7   L
503rd
504th
505th

353rd FG
66th FW
CLAIMS OF E/A DESTROYED
AIR 346½   GRD 440
TOTAL 786½
SQUADRON CODE AND COLOR
LH   350th FS   Yellow
YJ   351st FS   None
SX   352nd FS   Black
COMBAT: 12 Aug 43 to 25 Apr 45
P-47 12 Aug. 43
P-51 2 Oct. 44
Apr. 44
Oct. 44
Dec. 44
RUDDERS Nov. 44
LH   L
350th
351st
352nd

357th FG
66th FW
CLAIMS OF E/A DESTROYED
AIR 592   GRD 120
TOTAL 712
SQUADRON CODE AND COLOR
G4   362nd FS   White/None
B6   363rd FS   Red
C5   364th FS   Yellow
COMBAT: 11 Feb 44 to 25 Apr 45
P-51 11 Feb. 44
Apr. 44
RUDDERS Nov. 44
G4   L
362nd
363rd
364th

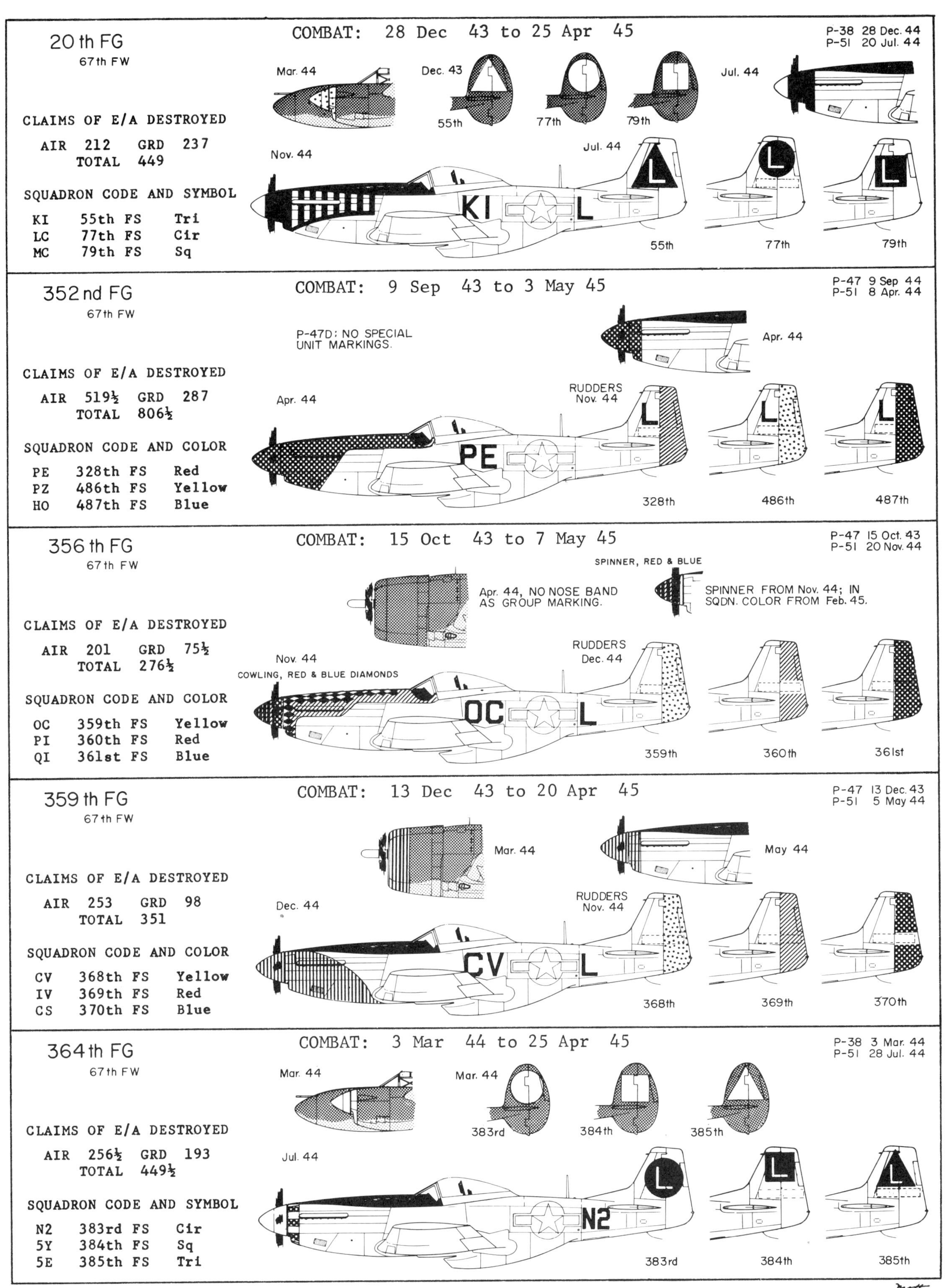


20th FG
67th FW

COMBAT: 28 Dec 43 to 25 Apr 45

P-38 28 Dec. 44
P-51 20 Jul. 44

Mar. 44
Dec. 43
55th
77th
79th
Jul. 44

CLAIMS OF E/A DESTROYED

AIR 212   GRD 237
TOTAL 449

Nov. 44
Jul. 44

SQUADRON CODE AND SYMBOL

KI   55th FS   Tri
LC   77th FS   Cir
MC   79th FS   Sq

KI
L
55th
77th
79th

352nd FG
67th FW

COMBAT: 9 Sep 43 to 3 May 45

P-47 9 Sep 44
P-51 8 Apr. 44

P-47D: NO SPECIAL
UNIT MARKINGS.

Apr. 44

CLAIMS OF E/A DESTROYED

AIR 519½   GRD 287
TOTAL 806½

Apr. 44

RUDDERS
Nov. 44

SQUADRON CODE AND COLOR

PE   328th FS   Red
PZ   486th FS   Yellow
HO   487th FS   Blue

PE
L
328th
486th
487th

356th FG
67th FW

COMBAT: 15 Oct 43 to 7 May 45

P-47 15 Oct. 43
P-51 20 Nov. 44

SPINNER, RED & BLUE

Apr. 44, NO NOSE BAND
AS GROUP MARKING.

SPINNER FROM Nov. 44; IN
SQDN. COLOR FROM Feb. 45.

CLAIMS OF E/A DESTROYED

AIR 201   GRD 75½
TOTAL 276½

Nov. 44
COWLING, RED & BLUE DIAMONDS

RUDDERS
Dec. 44

SQUADRON CODE AND COLOR

OC   359th FS   Yellow
PI   360th FS   Red
QI   361st FS   Blue

OC
L
359th
360th
361st

359th FG
67th FW

COMBAT: 13 Dec 43 to 20 Apr 45

P-47 13 Dec. 43
P-51 5 May 44

Mar. 44
May 44

CLAIMS OF E/A DESTROYED

AIR 253   GRD 98
TOTAL 351

Dec. 44

RUDDERS
Nov. 44

SQUADRON CODE AND COLOR

CV   368th FS   Yellow
IV   369th FS   Red
CS   370th FS   Blue

CV
L
368th
369th
370th

364th FG
67th FW

COMBAT: 3 Mar 44 to 25 Apr 45

P-38 3 Mar. 44
P-51 28 Jul. 44

Mar. 44
Mar. 44
383rd
384th
385th

CLAIMS OF E/A DESTROYED

AIR 256½   GRD 193
TOTAL 449½

Jul. 44

SQUADRON CODE AND SYMBOL

N2   383rd FS   Cir
5Y   384th FS   Sq
5E   385th FS   Tri

N2
L
383rd
384th
385th

matt

Left, Republic P-47M, 44-21117, of the 56th Fighter Group in the dark green and light grey shadow shading with yellow code and aircraft letter of the 62nd Fighter Squadron, and right, P-47D of the 355th Fighter Group in early 1944.

"Maggie V" a P-47D of the 353rd Fighter Group at Beny-sur-Mer, France on 30 June 1944. (AAF)

A 78th Fighter Group P-47D at Plumetot, France, also on the 30th of June 1944. (AAF)

Lockheed P-38J of the 364th Fighter Group after crash landing in England in April or May 1944. (Ray E. Bowers)

"Murph III" a P-38J of the 20th Fighter Group, KI-V, warming up for a mission in the spring of 1944. (Royal D. Frey)

Mustangs of the 359th Fighter Group with "X-terminator" in the foreground. At upper left are a P-51D, a P-51C with Malcolm hood and a P-51B, coded IV-T, G and H. (Bill Hess)

Flight of 357th Fighter Group P-51D Mustangs painted with dark green upper surfaces and grey undersurfaces, plus Invasion Stripes. (Phil Yant)

Mustangs of the 361st FG, including War Weary P-51B, above left; of the 353rd FG, LH-Q, above right; of the 355th FG, Col. Claiborne Kinnard's WR-A, below left; of the 479th FG, Lt. Harold L. Stotts' "The Yakima Chief", below right.

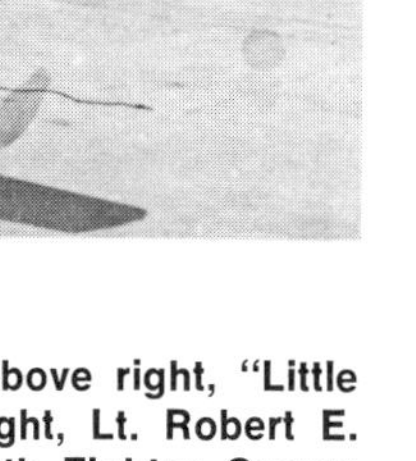

Above left, P-51D of the 4th Fighter Group; above right, "Little Lady" a P-51D of the 20th Fighter Group; right, Lt. Robert E. Barnhart and his "Margie Darling" of the 356th Fighter Group; and below, a P-51B of the 339th Fighter Group. (USAF, Royal D. Frey, Ray E. Bowers)

From mid-1944 each Eighth Air Division had a Scouting Force with P-51s provided by: 364th FG, 385th FS, right, with all tail surfaces outlined in red and red spinner, 1st Scouting Force; 355th FG, 354th FS, with green upper half and white lower half nose band, 2nd Scouting Force; 55th FG, 338th FS, above, with red and white checkerboard rudder and red outlined fin, 3rd Scouting Force. (William T. Searby, who flew CL-I, and USAF)

During early operations, Eighth bombers carried no unit markings. Then, from November 1942, the heavies began the use of an aircraft letter, on the vertical fin in yellow. From December 1942, squadron codes in combination with the aircraft letter, both on the fuselage in grey, came into use on the Fortresses. Usually the squadron code was placed forward of the national insignia and the aircraft letter aft, with the latter also remaining on the vertical fin. Later, with the advent of the barred national insignia, some groups varied the placement of the squadron code/aircraft letter combination on the fuselage. Some grouped the three letters together forward or aft of the national insignia. Another split the three between the two letters of the code. Others placed the squadron code only on the rear sides of the fuselage. And several groups never employed squadron codes. With the advent of natural metal finish B-17s, the squadron codes and aircraft letter were in black.

Liberators began use of squadron codes in March 1944, placing them on the aft sides of the fuselage, with the aircraft letter remaining on the fin in most cases. The 3rd Division's B-24s of the 486th and 487th BG's did the same, but repeated the aircraft letter on the sides of the fuselage forward of the national insignia. The 3rd's other three B-24 groups never used squadron codes, having only an aircraft letter on the vertical fins of their Libs.

As a further aid to identification, each Bomb Wing/Division initiated the use of a geometric symbol on the vertical tail and upper right wing — from June 1943 for the B-17s and from August 1943 for the B-24s. These were a triangle for the 1st Bomb Wing/Division, circle for the 2nd, square for the 4th/3rd. Within this symbol a group letter was placed — a black letter in a white symbol on OD planes, a white letter in a black symbol on NMF planes.

From late 1943, most Liberator units began the use of a bar or plus sign in conjunction with the aircraft letter as a further means of squadron identification.

Thus by the spring of 1944, Eighth bombers were identified by a Division symbol, a Group letter, a squadron code and an aircraft letter (plus a squadron sign on B-24s).

From the end of April 1944, the Liberators changed over to Wing colored outer vertical tail surfaces—black 2nd CBW, white 14th CBW, yellow 20th CBW, red 96th CBW, and green 95th CBW — with a contrasting band (black or white) across them, vertically, horizontally or diagonally, to denote the group within the Wing, and with the aircraft letter (and sign) on the band. The squadron code remained on the rear sides of the fuselage.

From July 1944, Fortress Wings employed distinctive Wing tail markings — red tails 1st CBW, horizontal tail band in group color 40th CBW, enlarged triangle in group color 41st CBW, diagonal tail band in group color 94th CBW, yellow tails and group color bands on rear fuselage 4th CBW (Feb 1945), vertical tail band in group color 13th CBW (Jan 1945), twin horizontal tail bands in group color 45th CBW (Jan 1945), red tail portions 93rd CBW.

Several B-17 Wings also employed wing markings — red wing tips 1st CBW, chevron on upper right and lower left wing in group color or colors 4th CBW, diagonal wing band in group color on upper right and lower left wing 13th CBW, twin chordwise bands in group color on upper right and lower left wing 45th CBW, chordwise red band around each wing and each horizontal tail 93rd CBW.

Finally, squadron colors were applied to many Fortresses from about July 1944. The color was applied either to the cowl ring, the propeller hub, the tail tip or as a band on the nose. In the case of the 493rd Bomb Group, a single letter to identify each squadron was placed on the sides of the fuselage amidships. Only two Liberator groups employed squadron colors, applied to the cowl rings.

The basic unit markings applied to Eighth B-17s and B-24s — from mid-1943 — are shown on the following pages. Presentation is by wing assignment.

**Nose art on bombers of the 1st, 2nd and 3rd Divisions.**

## 91st BG
1st CBW



COMBAT:  7 Nov 42 to 25 Apr 45

340 Missions

from Jul 44

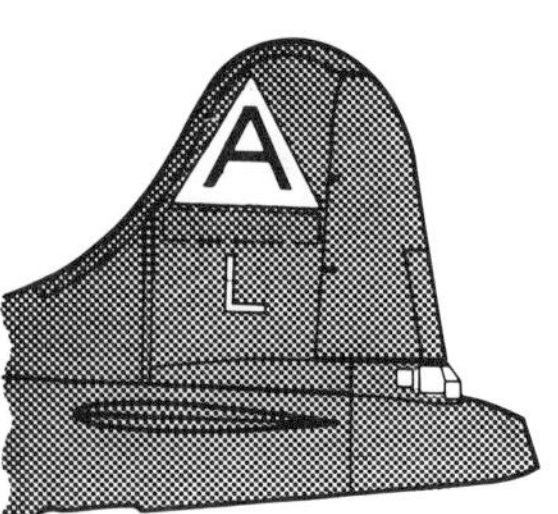
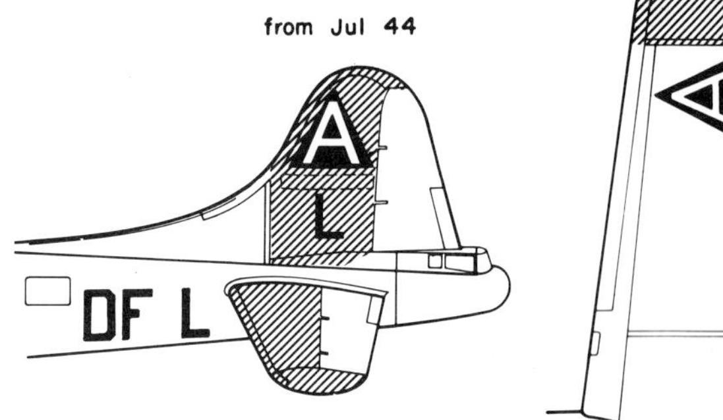



SQUADRON CODE

|  |  |
|------|----------|
| LG | 322nd BS |
| OR | 323rd BS |
| DF | 324th BS |
| LL | 401st BS |

---

## 381st BG
1st CBW

COMBAT:  22 Jun 43 to 25 Apr 45

297 Missions

from Jul 44

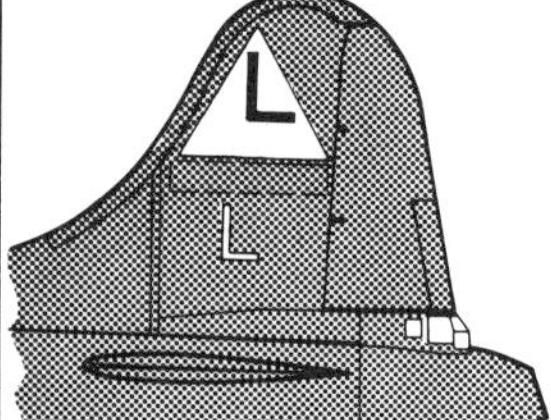
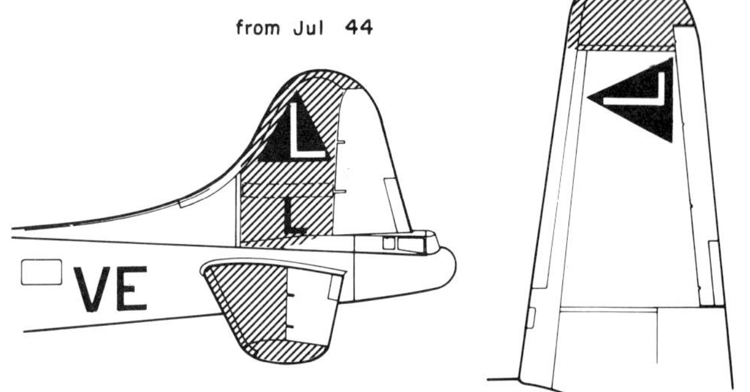



SQUADRON CODE

|  |  |
|------|----------|
| VE | 532nd BS |
| VP | 533rd BS |
| GD | 534th BS |
| MS | 535th BS |

---

## 398th BG
1st CBW

COMBAT:  6 May 44 to 25 Apr 45

195 Missions

from Jul 44

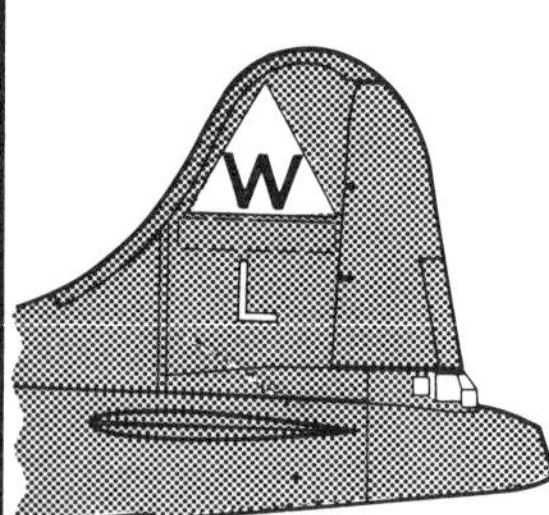
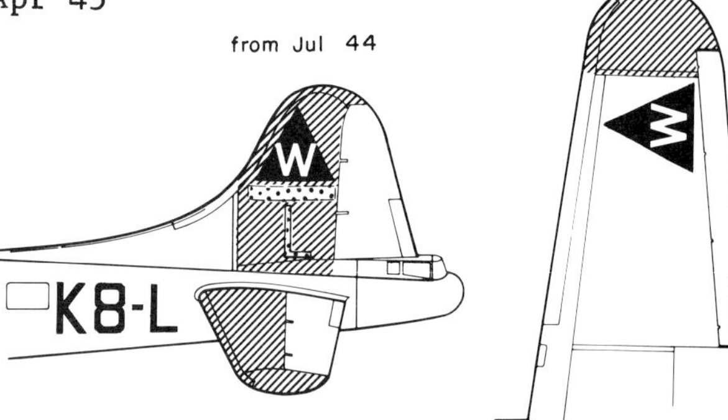



SQUADRON CODE

|  |  |
|------|----------|
| N8 | 600th BS |
| 3O | 601st BS |
| K8 | 602nd BS |
| N7 | 603rd BS |

---

## 92nd BG
40th CBW

COMBAT:  6 Sep 42 to 9 Oct 42 and
14 May 43 to 25 Apr 45

310 Missions

from Aug 44

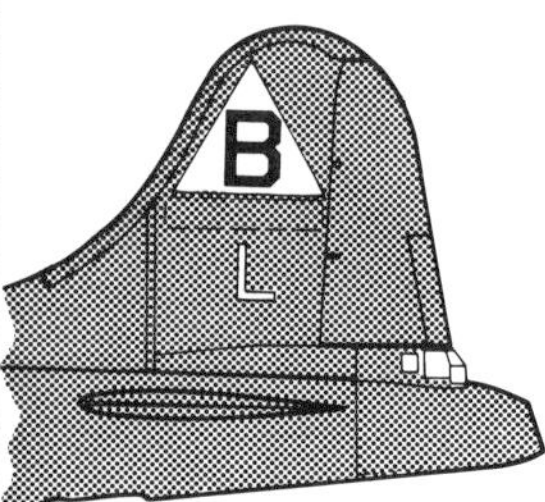
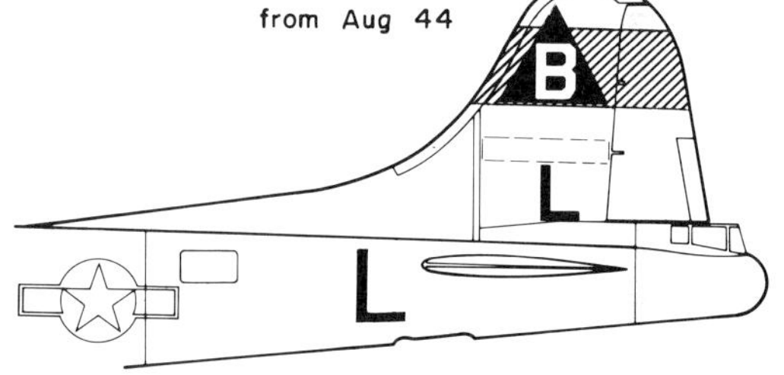



SQUADRON CODE

|  |  |
|------|----------|
| NV | 325th BS |
| JW | 326th BS |
| UX | 327th BS |
| PY | 407th BS |

---

## 305th BG
40th CBW

COMBAT:  17 Nov 42 to 25 Apr 45

337 Missions

from Aug 44

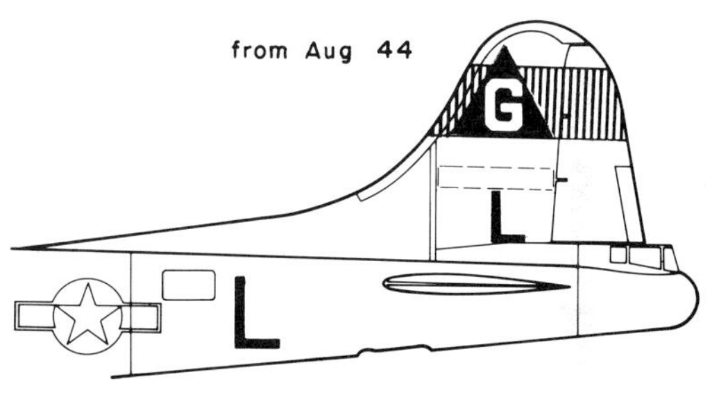



SQUADRON CODE

|  |  |
|------|----------|
| WF | 364th BS |
| XK | 365th BS |
| KY | 366th BS |
| JJ | 422nd BS |

# 306th BG
### 40th CBW

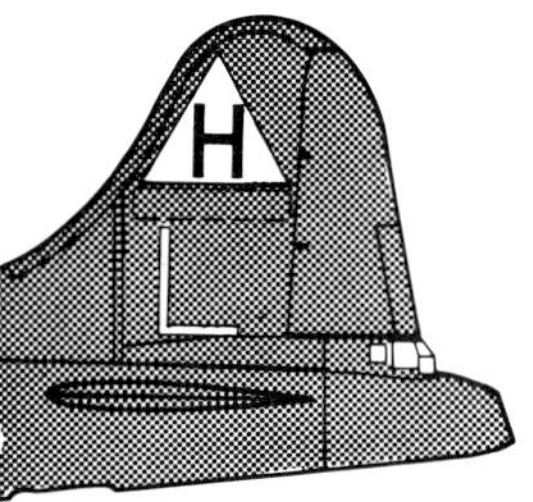

**COMBAT:** 9 Oct 42  19 Apr 45

342 Missions

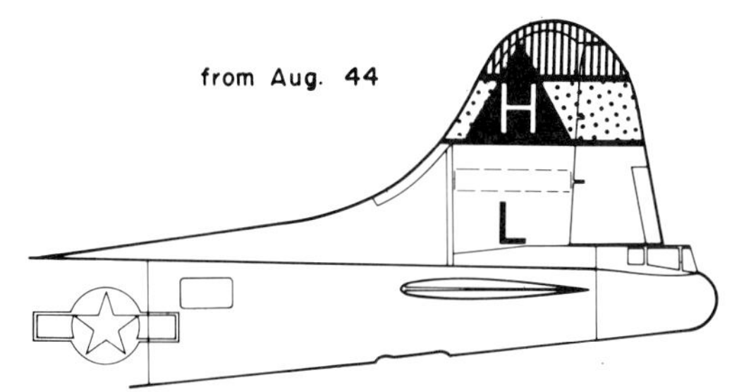

from Aug. 44

SQUADRON CODE & TAIL TIP COLOR
(to Apr 44)    (from Aug 44)

| GY | 367th BS | Red |
| BO | 368th BS | White |
| WW | 369th BS | Green |
| RD | 423rd BS | Blue |

---

# 303rd BG
### 41st CBW

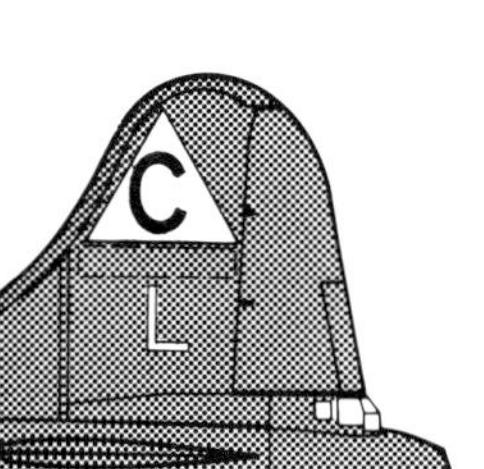

**COMBAT:** 17 Nov 42 to 25 Apr 45

364 Missions

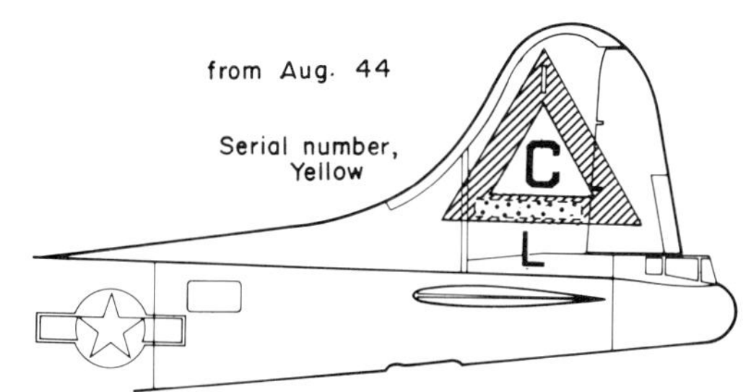

from Aug. 44

Serial number, Yellow

SQUADRON CODE & SQUADRON NO.

| VK | 358th BS | 1 |
| BN | 359th BS | 2 |
| PU | 360th BS | 3 |
| GN | 427th BS | 4 |

---

# 379th BG
### 41st CBW

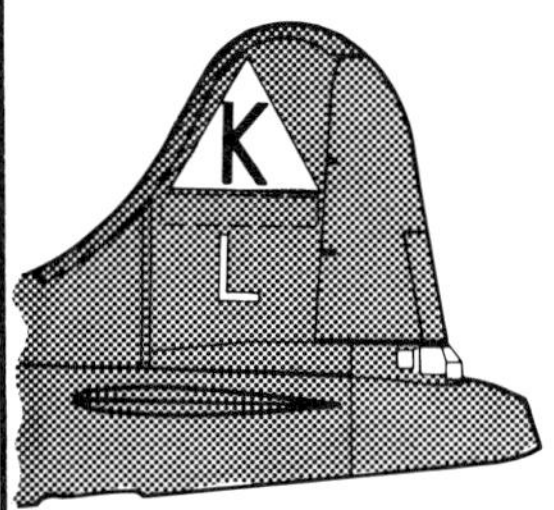

**COMBAT:** 29 May 43 to 25 Apr 45

330 Missions

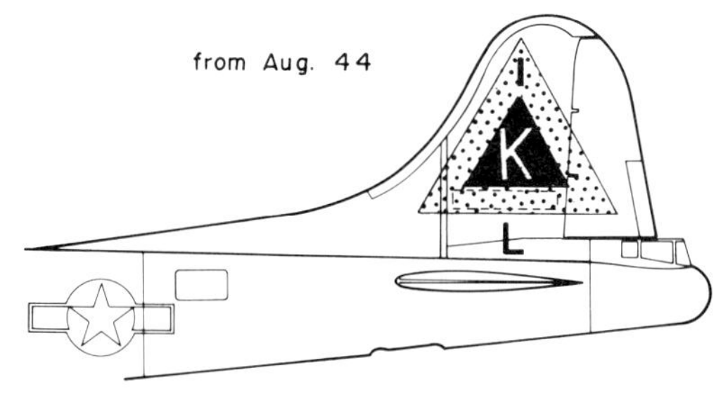

from Aug. 44

SQUADRON CODE & SQUADRON NO.

| WA | 524th BS | 1 |
| FR | 525th BS | 2 |
| LF | 526th BS | 3 |
| FO | 527th BS | 4 |

---

# 384th BG
### 41st CBW

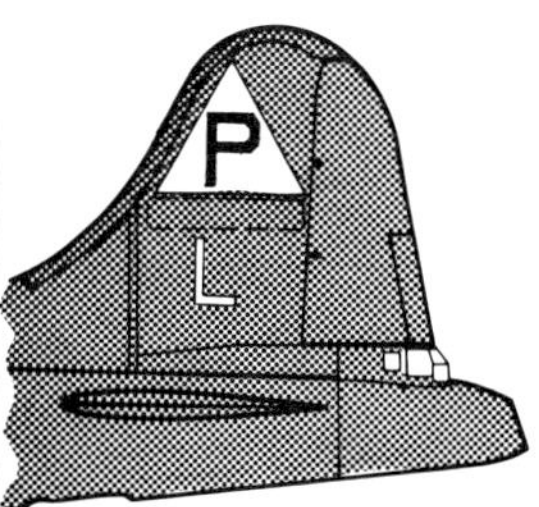

**COMBAT:** 22 Jun 43 to 25 Apr 45

314 Missions

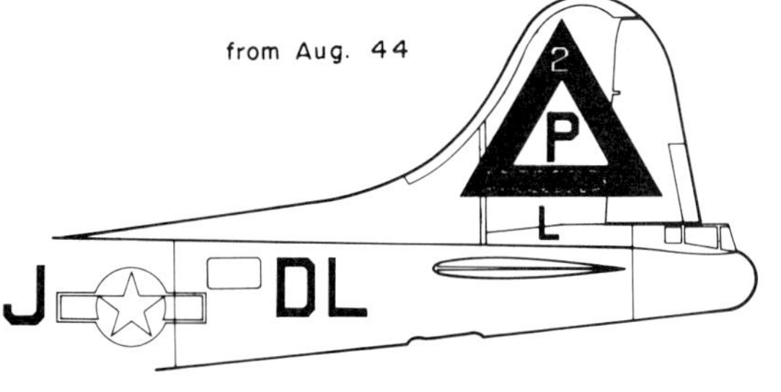

from Aug. 44

SQUADRON CODE & SQUADRON NO.

| SU | 544th BS | 1 |
| JD | 545th BS | 2 |
| BK | 546th BS | 3 |
| SO | 547th BS | 4 |

---

# 351st BG
### 94th CBW

from Dec. 43

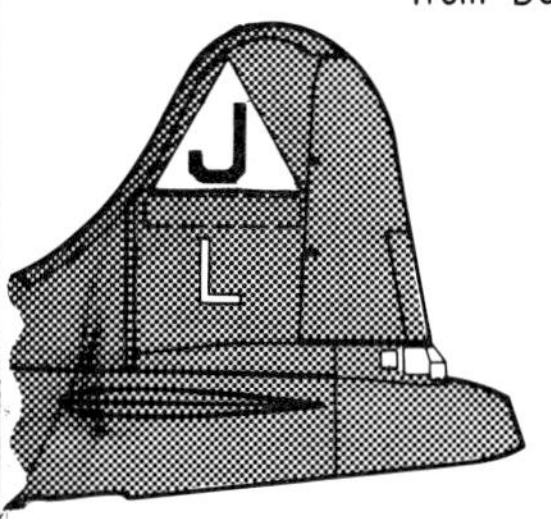

**COMBAT:** 14 May 43 to 25 Apr 45

311 Missions

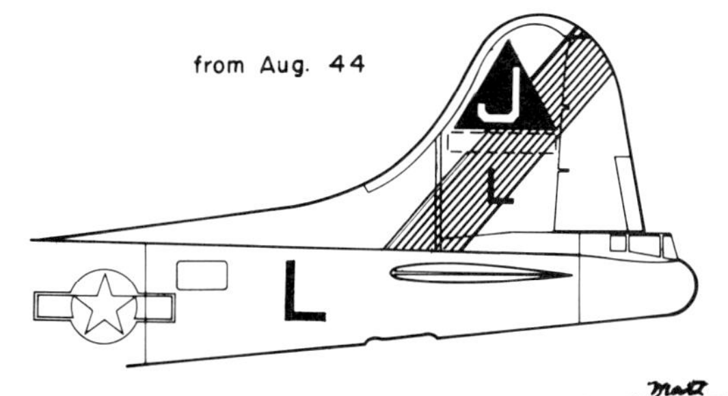

from Aug. 44

SQUADRON CODE

| YB | 508th BS |
| RQ | 509th BS |
| TU | 510th BS |
| DS | 511th BS |

## 401st BG

94th CBW

*from Dec 43*

**COMBAT:** 26 Nov 43 to 20 Apr 45

254 Missions

*from Aug 44*

**SQUADRON CODE**

| | |
|---|---|
| SC | 612th BS |
| IN | 613th BS |
| IW | 614th BS |
| IY | 615th BS |

---

## 457th BG

94th CBW

**COMBAT:** 21 Feb 44 to 20 Apr 45

236 Missions

*from Aug 44*

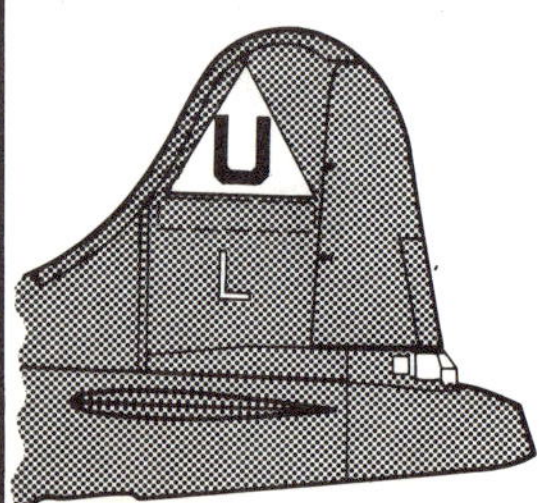

**SQUADRON CODE & PROP HUB COLOR**

| | | |
|---|---|---|
| NONE | 748th BS | Red |
| NONE | 749th BS | Blue |
| NONE | 750th BS | White |
| NONE | 751st BS | Yellow |

---

## 94th BG

4th CBW

**COMBAT:** 13 May 43 to 21 Apr 45

324 Missions

*from Feb 45*

*late 44* →

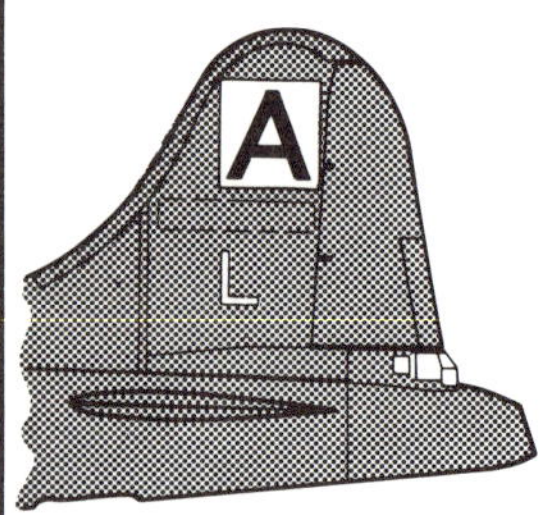

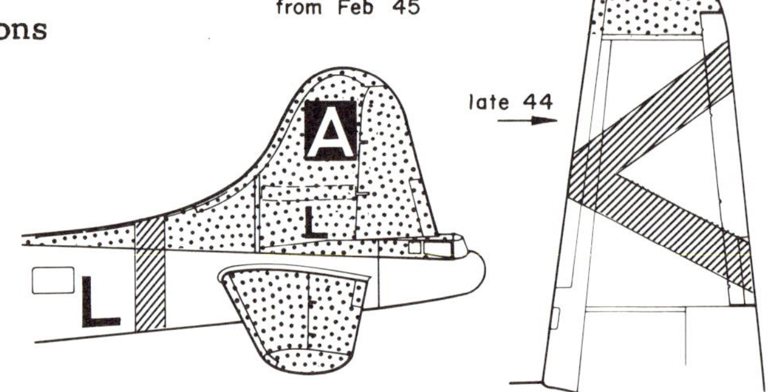



**SQUADRON CODE & COWL COLOR**

| | | |
|---|---|---|
| QE | 331st BS | Blue |
| XM | 332nd BS | Red |
| TS | 333rd BS | Green |
| GL | 410th BS | Yellow |

---

## 385th BG

4th CBW

*to Feb 45*

**COMBAT:** 17 Jul 43 to 20 Apr 45

296 Missions

*from late 44* →

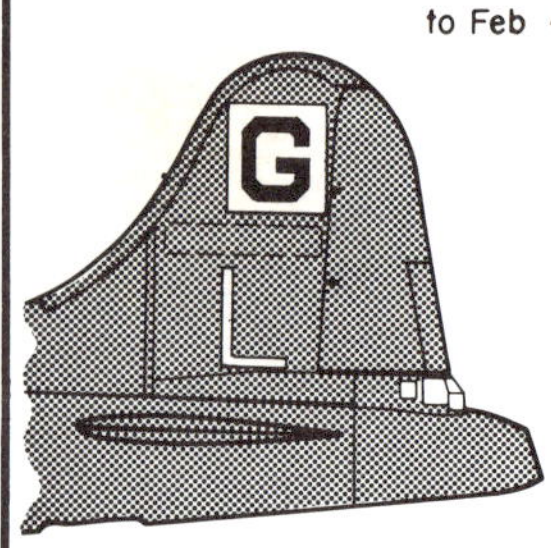

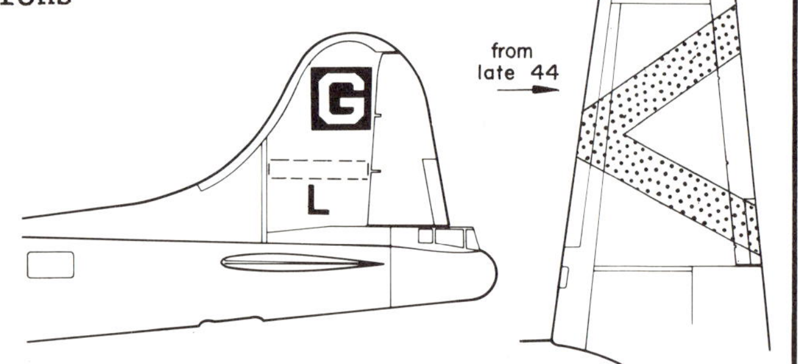



**SQUADRON CODE & PROP HUB COLOR**

(not used)  (from '43)

| | | |
|---|---|---|
| GX | 548th BS | Blue |
| XA | 549th BS | Yellow |
| SG | 550th BS | Red |
| HR | 551st BS | Green |

---

## 447th BG

4th CBW

**COMBAT:** 24 Dec 43 to 21 Apr 45

258 Missions

*from Feb 45*

*late 44* →

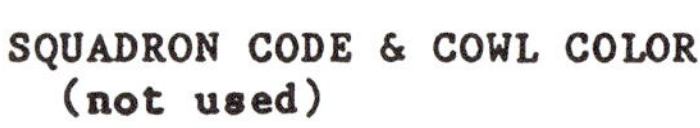

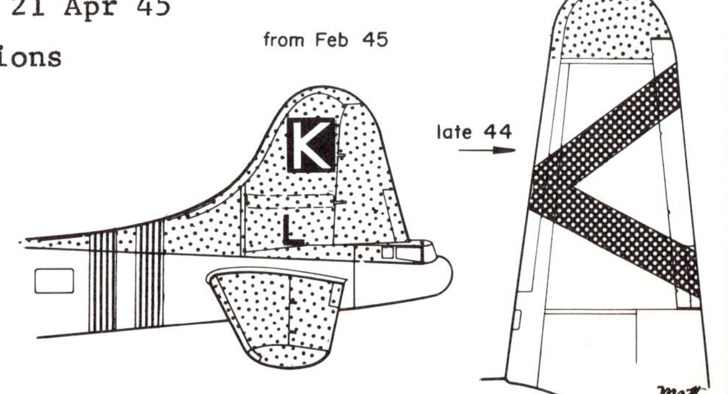



**SQUADRON CODE & COWL COLOR**

(not used)

| | | |
|---|---|---|
| CQ | 708th BS | Yellow |
| IE | 709th BS | White |
| IJ | 710th BS | Red |
| IR | 711th BS | Blue |

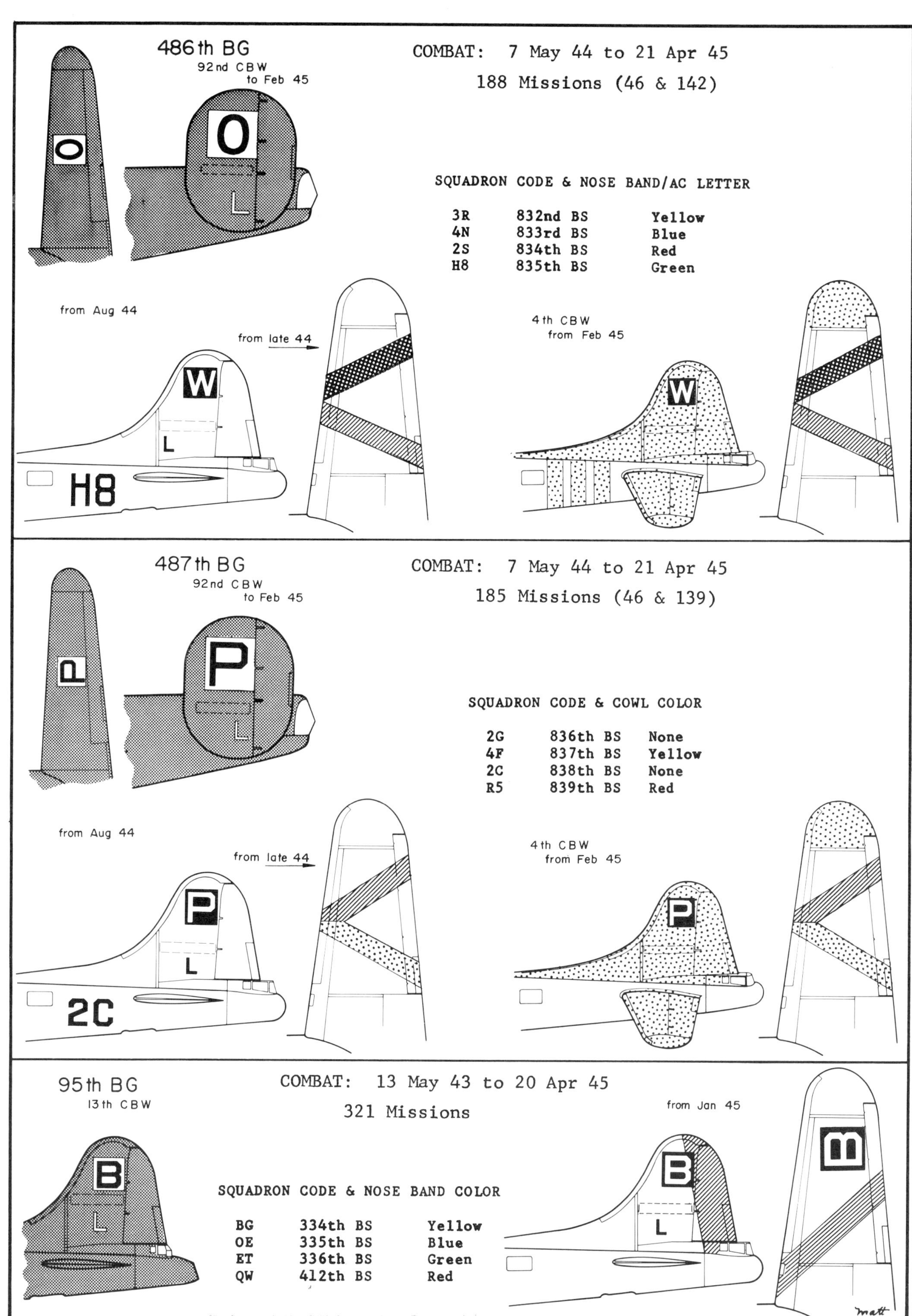

486th BG
92nd CBW
to Feb 45
COMBAT:  7 May 44 to 21 Apr 45
188 Missions (46 & 142)

O
O
L

SQUADRON CODE & NOSE BAND/AC LETTER

3R      832nd BS      Yellow
4N      833rd BS      Blue
2S      834th BS      Red
H8      835th BS      Green

from Aug 44
from late 44
W
L
H8
4th CBW
from Feb 45
W

487th BG
92nd CBW
to Feb 45
COMBAT:  7 May 44 to 21 Apr 45
185 Missions (46 & 139)

P
P
L

SQUADRON CODE & COWL COLOR

2G      836th BS      None
4F      837th BS      Yellow
2C      838th BS      None
R5      839th BS      Red

from Aug 44
from late 44
P
L
2C
4th CBW
from Feb 45
P

95th BG
13th CBW
COMBAT:  13 May 43 to 20 Apr 45
321 Missions
from Jan 45
B

SQUADRON CODE & NOSE BAND COLOR

BG      334th BS      Yellow
OE      335th BS      Blue
ET      336th BS      Green
QW      412th BS      Red

B
L
B
L
matt

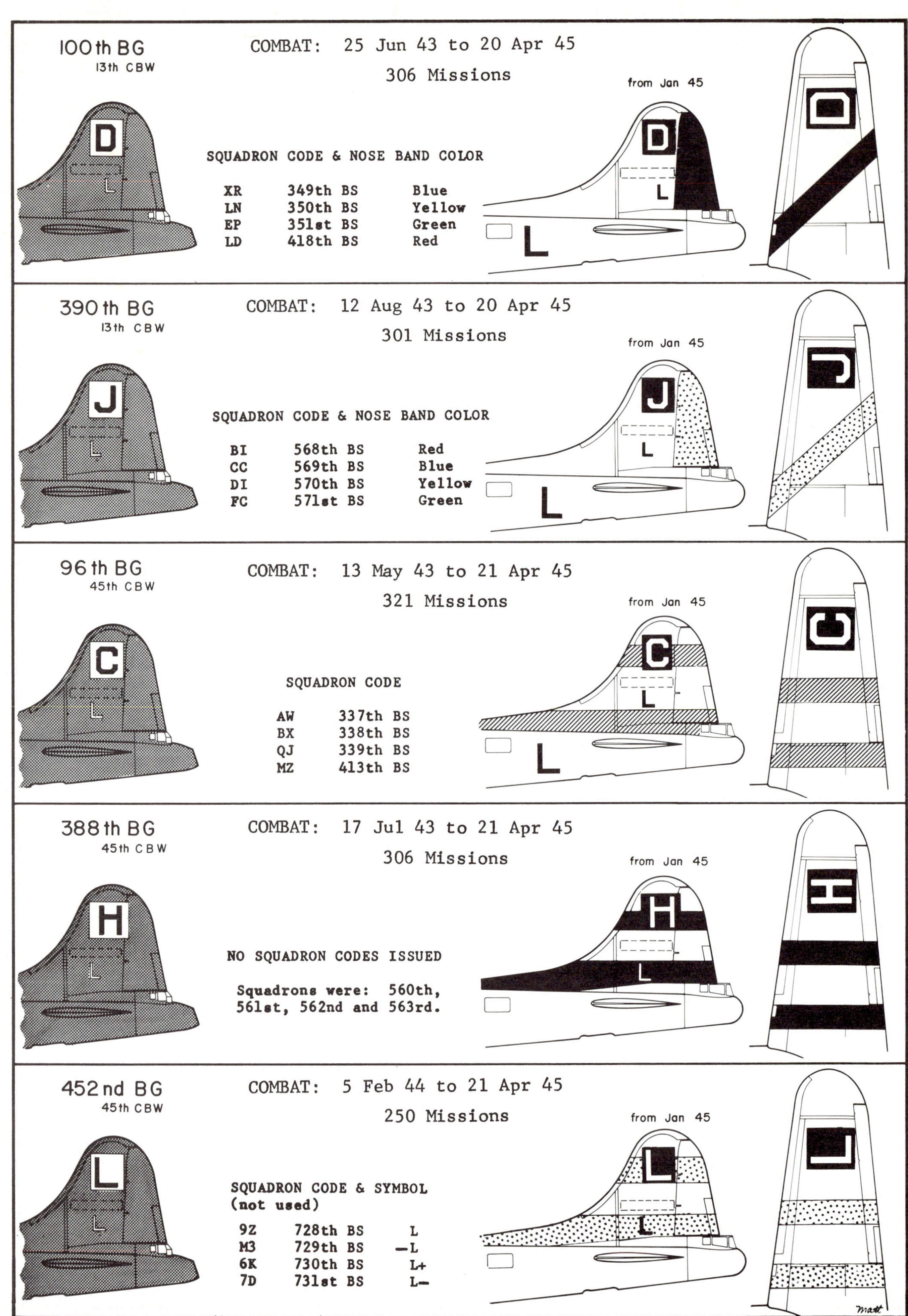

100th BG
13th CBW

COMBAT:  25 Jun 43 to 20 Apr 45

306 Missions

from Jan 45

SQUADRON CODE & NOSE BAND COLOR

XR    349th BS    Blue
LN    350th BS    Yellow
EP    351st BS    Green
LD    418th BS    Red

390th BG
13th CBW

COMBAT:  12 Aug 43 to 20 Apr 45

301 Missions

from Jan 45

SQUADRON CODE & NOSE BAND COLOR

BI    568th BS    Red
CC    569th BS    Blue
DI    570th BS    Yellow
FC    571st BS    Green

96th BG
45th CBW

COMBAT:  13 May 43 to 21 Apr 45

321 Missions

from Jan 45

SQUADRON CODE

AW    337th BS
BX    338th BS
QJ    339th BS
MZ    413th BS

388th BG
45th CBW

COMBAT:  17 Jul 43 to 21 Apr 45

306 Missions

from Jan 45

NO SQUADRON CODES ISSUED

Squadrons were:  560th,
561st, 562nd and 563rd.

452nd BG
45th CBW

COMBAT:  5 Feb 44 to 21 Apr 45

250 Missions

from Jan 45

SQUADRON CODE & SYMBOL
(not used)

9Z    728th BS    L
M3    729th BS    —L
6K    730th BS    L+
7D    731st BS    L—

Matt

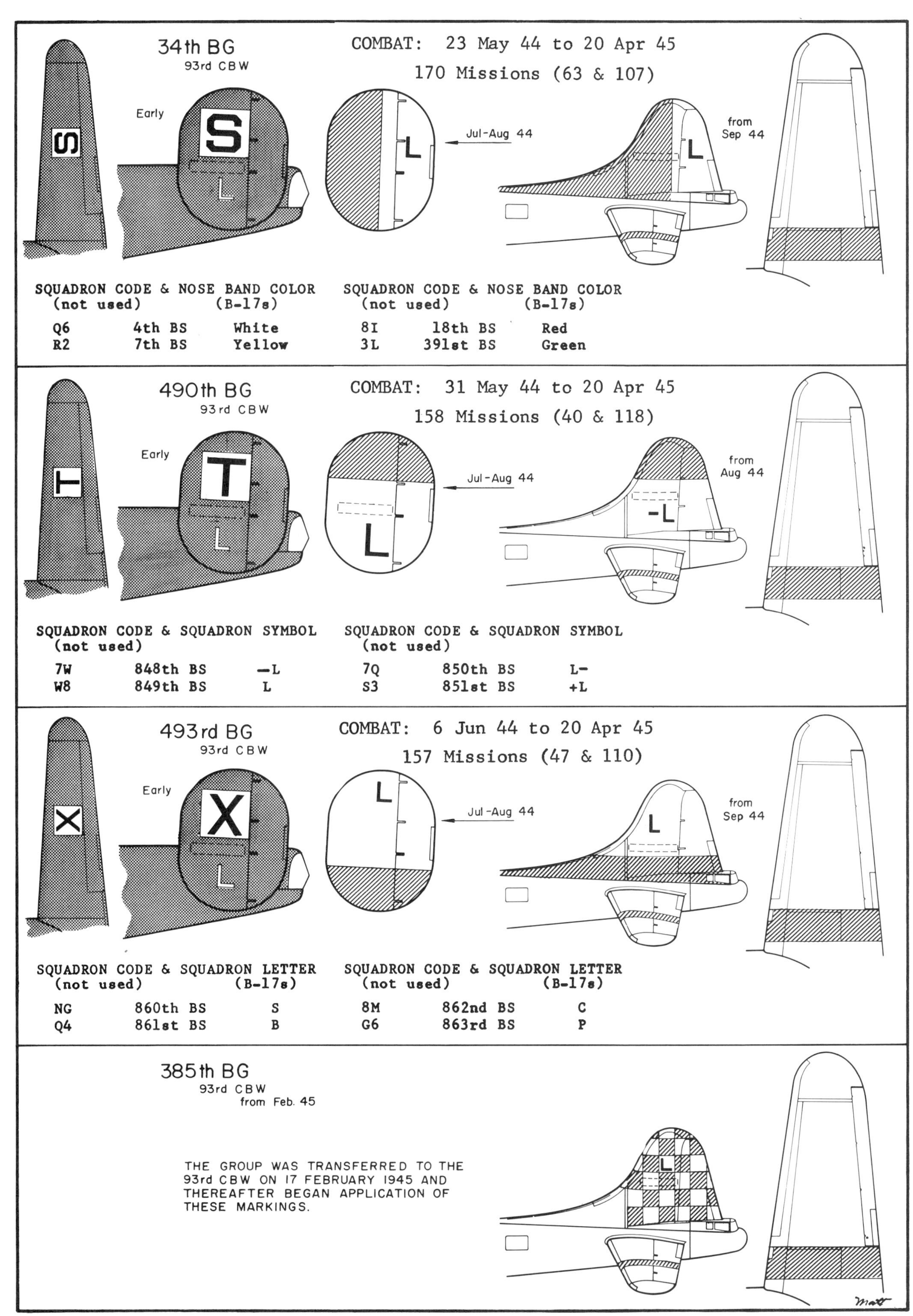

34th BG
93rd CBW
COMBAT: 23 May 44 to 20 Apr 45
170 Missions (63 & 107)
Early
S
S
L
L
Jul-Aug 44
L
from Sep 44
L

SQUADRON CODE & NOSE BAND COLOR
(not used)        (B-17s)
Q6    4th BS      White
R2    7th BS      Yellow

SQUADRON CODE & NOSE BAND COLOR
(not used)        (B-17s)
8I    18th BS     Red
3L    391st BS    Green

490th BG
93rd CBW
COMBAT: 31 May 44 to 20 Apr 45
158 Missions (40 & 118)
Early
T
T
L
L
Jul-Aug 44
L
from Aug 44
-L

SQUADRON CODE & SQUADRON SYMBOL
(not used)
7W    848th BS    —L
W8    849th BS    L

SQUADRON CODE & SQUADRON SYMBOL
(not used)
7Q    850th BS    L—
S3    851st BS    +L

493rd BG
93rd CBW
COMBAT: 6 Jun 44 to 20 Apr 45
157 Missions (47 & 110)
Early
X
X
L
L
Jul-Aug 44
L
from Sep 44
L

SQUADRON CODE & SQUADRON LETTER
(not used)        (B-17s)
NG    860th BS    S
Q4    861st BS    B

SQUADRON CODE & SQUADRON LETTER
(not used)        (B-17s)
8M    862nd BS    C
G6    863rd BS    P

385th BG
93rd CBW
from Feb. 45

THE GROUP WAS TRANSFERRED TO THE
93rd CBW ON 17 FEBRUARY 1945 AND
THEREAFTER BEGAN APPLICATION OF
THESE MARKINGS.
L

Matt

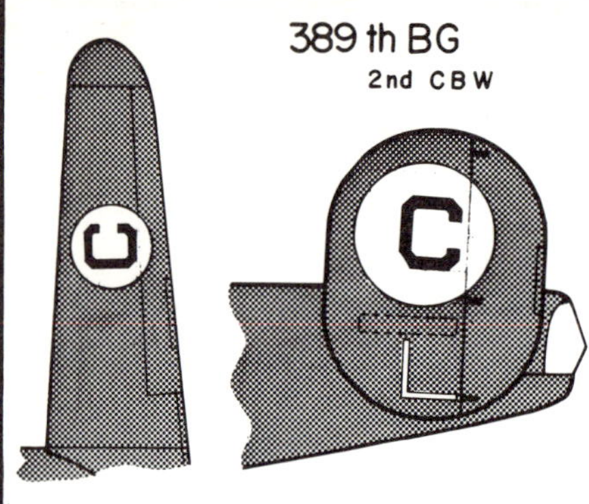

## 389th BG
### 2nd CBW

**COMBAT:  9 Jul 43 to 25 Apr 45**

**321 Missions (14 NA)**

from May 44

SQUADRON CODE & SYMBOL

| | | |
|---|---|---|
| YO * L | | 564th BS |
| EE * −L / $\overline{L}$ | | 565th BS |
| RR * L+ / $\underset{+}{L}$ | | 566th BS |
| HP * L− / $\underline{L}$ | | 567th BS |

---

## 445th BG
### 2nd CBW

**COMBAT:  13 Dec 43 to 25 Apr 45**

**280 Missions**

from May 44

SQUADRON CODE & SYMBOL

| | | |
|---|---|---|
| RN * L | | 700th BS |
| MK * $\overline{L}$ | | 701st BS |
| WV * $\underline{L}$ | | 702nd BS |
| IS * L+ | | 703rd BS |

---

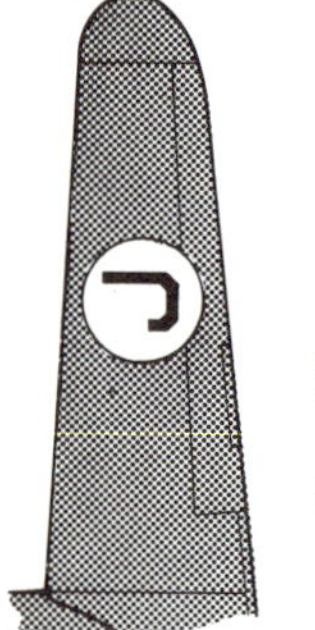
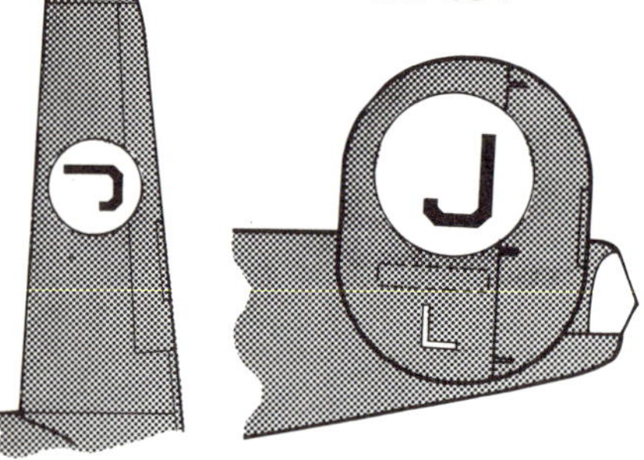

## 453rd BG
### 2nd CBW

**COMBAT:  5 Feb 44 to 12 Apr 45**

**259 Missions**

from May 44

SQUADRON CODE & SYMBOL

| | | |
|---|---|---|
| E3 * L | | 732nd BS |
| F8 * L+ | | 733rd BS |
| E8 * L− | | 734th BS |
| H6 * $\underline{L}$ | | 735th BS |

---

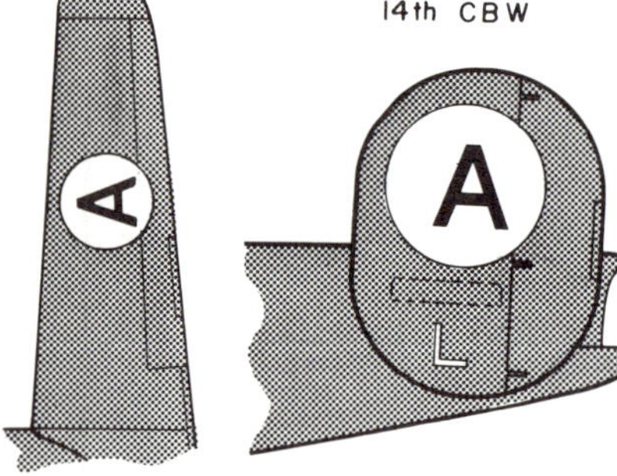

## 44th BG
### 14th CBW

**COMBAT:  7 Nov 42 to 25 Apr 45**

**343 Missions (18 NA)**

from May 44

SQUADRON CODE & SYMBOL

| | | |
|---|---|---|
| WQ * L | | 66th BS |
| NB * $\underline{L}$ | | 67th BS |
| GJ * $\overline{L}$ | | 68th BS |
| QK * L+ | | 506th BS |

---

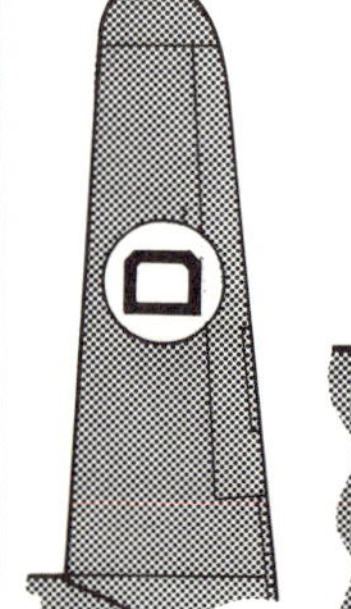
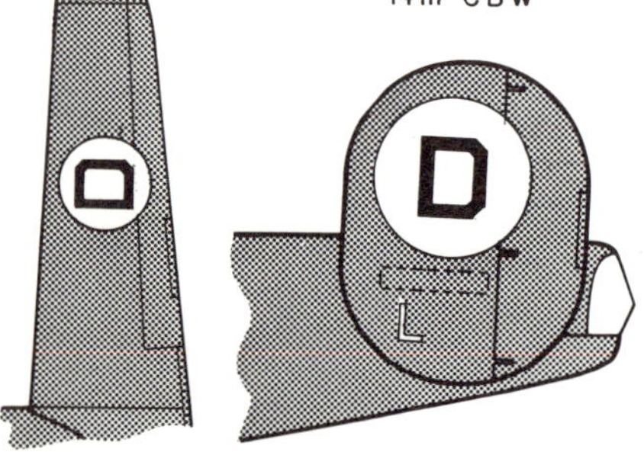

## 392nd BG
### 14th CBW

**COMBAT:  9 Sep 43 to 25 Apr 45**

**285 Missions**

from May 44

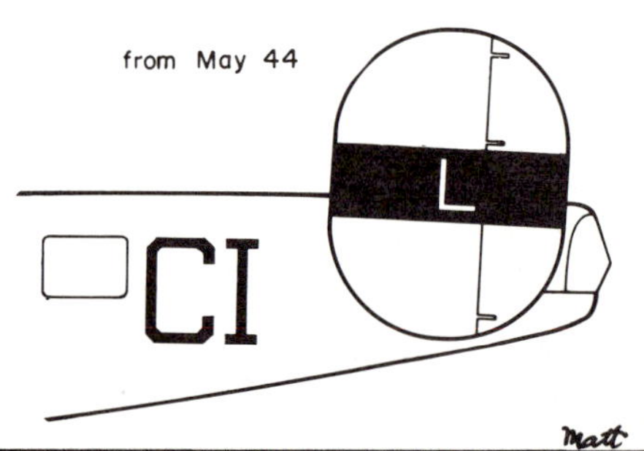

SQUADRON CODE & SYMBOL

| | | |
|---|---|---|
| CI * L | | 576th BS |
| DC * L+ | | 577th BS |
| EC * $\underline{L}$ | | 578th BS |
| GC * $\overline{L}$ | | 579th BS |

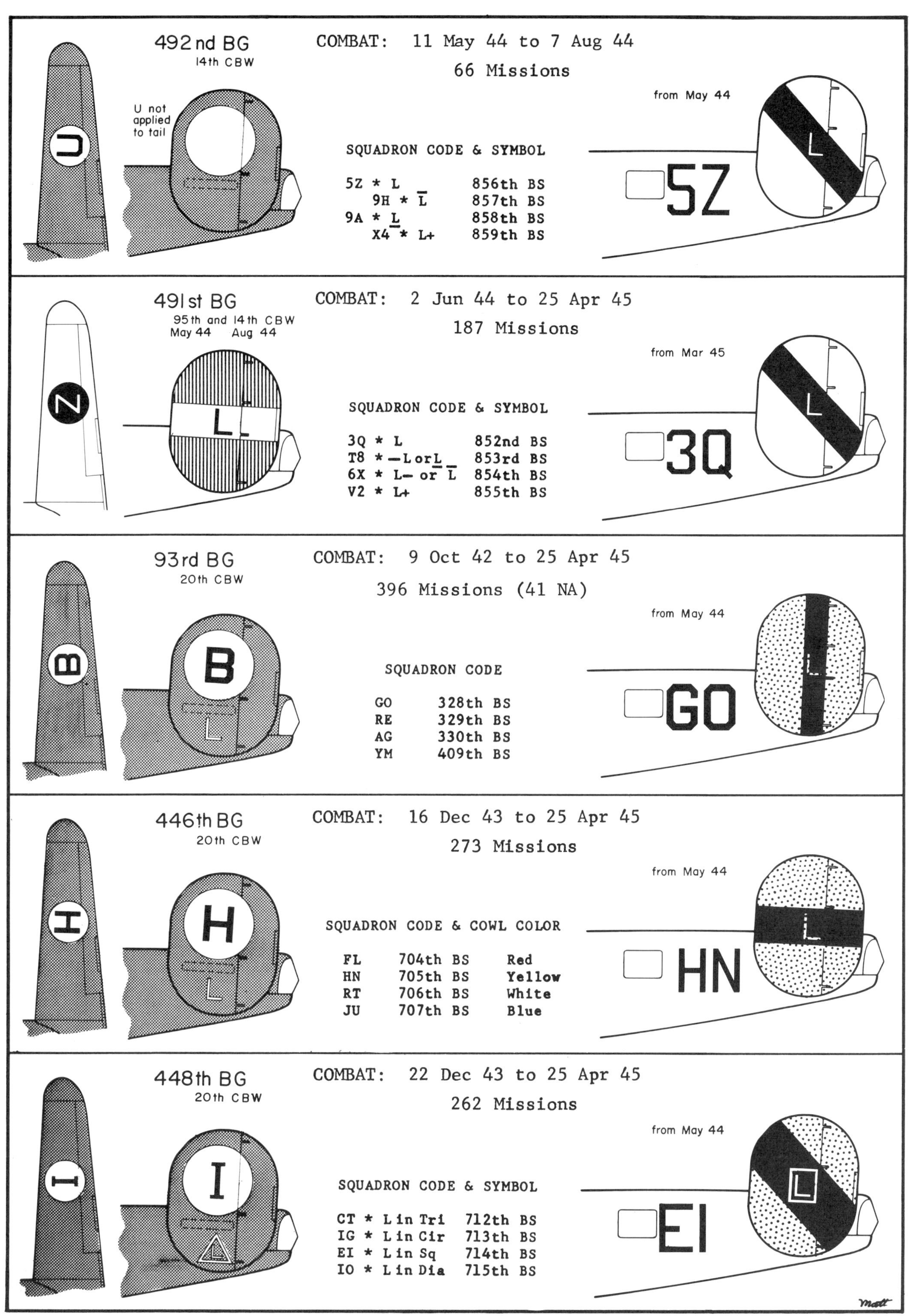

492nd BG
14th CBW
U not applied to tail
COMBAT: 11 May 44 to 7 Aug 44
66 Missions
from May 44
SQUADRON CODE & SYMBOL
5Z * L        856th BS
9H * L̄       857th BS
9A * L̲       858th BS
X4 * L+       859th BS
5Z

491st BG
95th and 14th CBW
May 44    Aug 44
COMBAT: 2 Jun 44 to 25 Apr 45
187 Missions
from Mar 45
SQUADRON CODE & SYMBOL
3Q * L        852nd BS
T8 * —L or L̲   853rd BS
6X * L— or L̄   854th BS
V2 * L+       855th BS
3Q

93rd BG
20th CBW
COMBAT: 9 Oct 42 to 25 Apr 45
396 Missions (41 NA)
from May 44
SQUADRON CODE
GO    328th BS
RE    329th BS
AG    330th BS
YM    409th BS
GO

446th BG
20th CBW
COMBAT: 16 Dec 43 to 25 Apr 45
273 Missions
from May 44
SQUADRON CODE & COWL COLOR
FL    704th BS    Red
HN    705th BS    Yellow
RT    706th BS    White
JU    707th BS    Blue
HN

448th BG
20th CBW
COMBAT: 22 Dec 43 to 25 Apr 45
262 Missions
from May 44
SQUADRON CODE & SYMBOL
CT * L in Tri   712th BS
IG * L in Cir   713th BS
EI * L in Sq    714th BS
IO * L in Dia   715th BS
EI
Matt

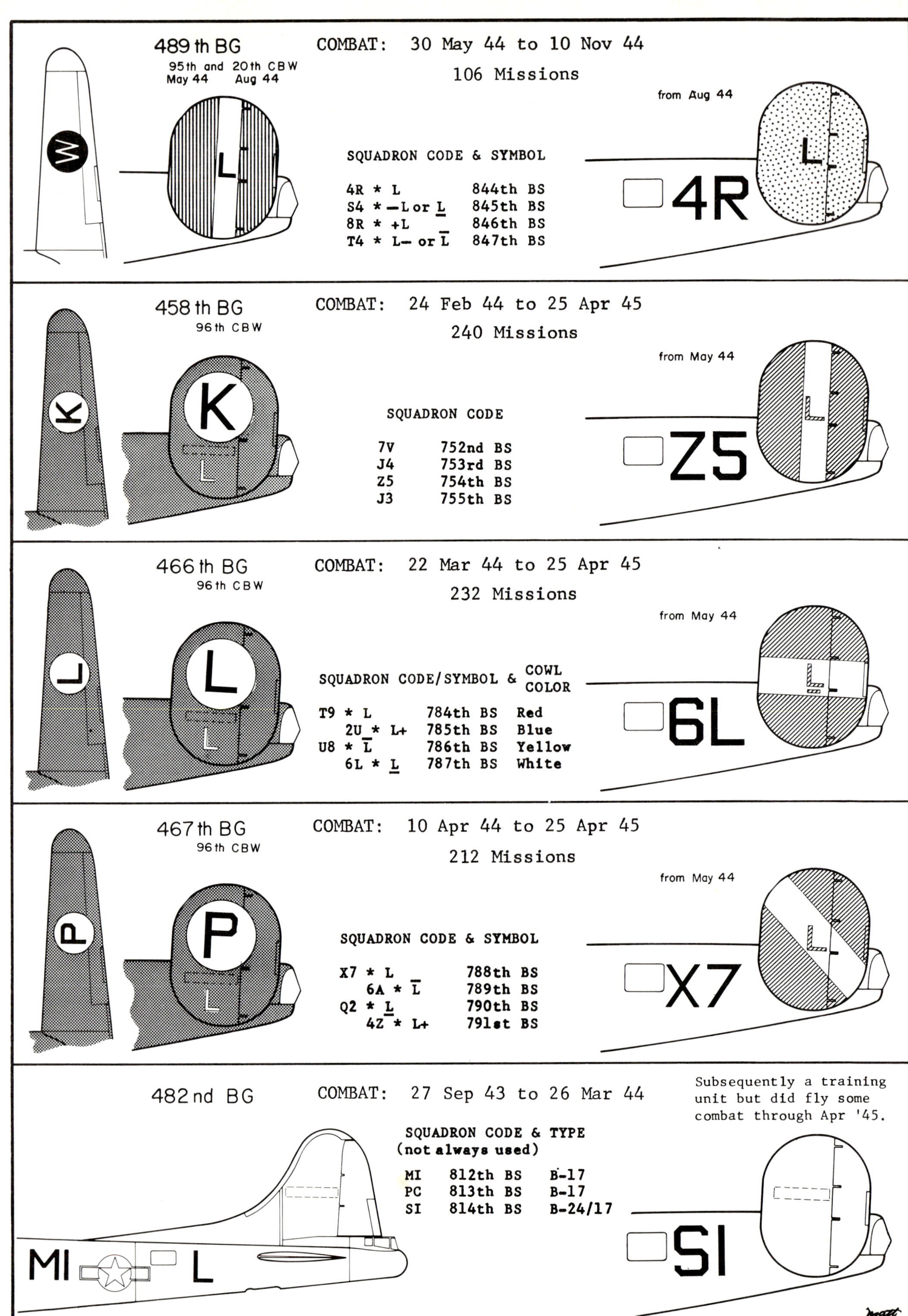

489th BG
95th and 20th CBW
May 44    Aug 44
W

COMBAT:    30 May 44 to 10 Nov 44
106 Missions

from Aug 44

SQUADRON CODE & SYMBOL

4R * L          844th BS
S4 * —L or L    845th BS
8R * +L         846th BS
T4 * L— or L    847th BS

4R

458th BG
96th CBW
K
K
L

COMBAT:    24 Feb 44 to 25 Apr 45
240 Missions

from May 44

SQUADRON CODE

7V    752nd BS
J4    753rd BS
Z5    754th BS
J3    755th BS

Z5

466th BG
96th CBW
L
L
L

COMBAT:    22 Mar 44 to 25 Apr 45
232 Missions

from May 44

SQUADRON CODE/SYMBOL & COWL COLOR

T9 * L    784th BS    Red
2U * L+   785th BS    Blue
U8 * L    786th BS    Yellow
6L * L    787th BS    White

6L

467th BG
96th CBW
P
P
L

COMBAT:    10 Apr 44 to 25 Apr 45
212 Missions

from May 44

SQUADRON CODE & SYMBOL

X7 * L    788th BS
6A * L    789th BS
Q2 * L    790th BS
4Z * L+   791st BS

X7

482nd BG

COMBAT:    27 Sep 43 to 26 Mar 44

Subsequently a training
unit but did fly some
combat through Apr '45.

SQUADRON CODE & TYPE
(not always used)

MI    812th BS    B-17
PC    813th BS    B-17
SI    814th BS    B-24/17

MI    L

SI

Above, "Hell's Angels Out of Chute 13" of the 401st Bomb Group on mission in the first half of 1944. Left, "Hell's Angels" of the 303rd Bomb Group, with 48 missions and a dozen enemy aircraft to its credit, is autographed by members of the Group in late 1943 before returning to the U.S. to help sell War Bonds. (Myke Jacobs and AAF via Harry Miller)

Pair of 92nd Bomb Group Fortresses on mission in late 1944 or early 1945. (AAF)

"Birmingham Blitzkrieg", a B-17E, 41-9100, which flew first Eighth mission with the 97th BG, eventually became a hack aircraft of the 379th Bomb Group, having white stripes added to its OD finish. (AAF)

A 384th Bomb Group Fortress, JD-L, at the moment of bombs away. (AAF)

Below, red tailed B-17G's of the 398th Bomb Group; next below, B-17G of the 351st Bomb Group; bottom, 306th Bomb Group B-17F. (Dwayne M. Tabatt, D. K. Griffiths, Ray Bowers)

Below, a 305th Bomb Group B-17F about to go down over Europe; next below, 457th Bomb Group B-17G; bottom, B-17G of the 384th Bomb Group. (AAF, Ken Blakebrough, Gus Radloff)

Liberators of the
446th Bomb Group
on mission, with
B-24J, 42-50814,
in foreground.
(L. M. Lowry)

"Witchcraft", B-24H, 42-52534,
of the 467th Bomb Group which
flew on Group's first mission
and completed one hundred
missions without an abort,
ended the war with over 125
missions. (Allan Healy)

"That's All Brother" of the
492nd Bomb Group over the
target at Saarbrucken on 16
July 1944. (USAF)

"Gas Housemouse" a B-24H,
42-95050, of the 458th Bomb
Group at RAF Base at Man-
ston on 13 December 1944.
(USAF)

The B-24H, 42-51099, "Belle",
of the 466th Bomb Group at an
airfield on the Continent.
(William L. Swisher)

Liberators of the 392nd Bomb Group drop their bombs on a German target. In foreground is B-24M, 44-50545. (AAF)

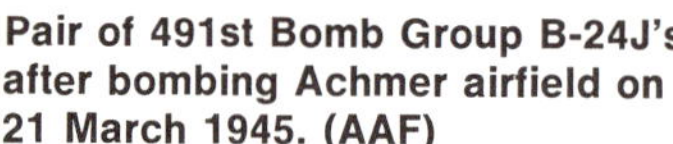

Pair of 491st Bomb Group B-24J's after bombing Achmer airfield on 21 March 1945. (AAF)

"Pistol Packin' Mama" of the 44th Bomb Group, a B-24D, on takeoff from Shipdham with the Group's Assembly Ship in front of hangar below. (AAF)

A B-24H of the 445th Bomb Group after crash landing in England as a result of battle damage over the Continent.

Left, B-24H of the 446th Bomb Group, and at right, a B-24H of the 489th Bomb Group. (AAF)

Above left, 453rd Bomb Group B-24H and above right, "Hello Natural" a B-24H, 41-29191, of the 448th Bomb Group. Below left, an H model Lib, 42-94918, of the 493rd Bomb Group and below right, B-24J, 42-50613 of the 34th Bomb Group.    Bottom left and right, B-24H, June 1944, and B-17G, December 1944, of the 486th Bomb Group. (AAF, William Swisher, R. H. Hodges)

Above, B-17G Fortresses of the 490th Bomb Group, and at left, a B-17F of the 385th Bomb Group. (Robert Louden and Ray E. Bowers)

Above and below, montage of early and later aircraft of the 96th Bomb Group. The B-17F below left, 42-5885, is "Kipling's Error the III" while the B-17G below right, 43-37716, "5 Grand", was the 5,000th B-17 built. (M. D. Wilson/C. Moschel)

A yellow tailed 94th Bomb Group Fortress with chin and ball turrets removed. (William T. Ashley)

A 487th Bomb Group B-17G with mismatched OD vertical fin on its bomb run. (AAF)

Glistening new B-17G of the 452nd Bomb Group in the last months of 1944. (AAF via Harry Miller)

From above left, 96th Group B-17G at Snetterton Heath in February 1945; 447th Bomb Group Fortress at Rattlesden in March 1944; B-17G of the 493rd Bomb Group in February 1945; squadron colored nose band on 100th Group Fortress. And at right, proof that all art was not on the nose, is "Tail Bait" a B-17F of the 95th Bomb Group in mid-1943. (AAF and Cliff Manella via Thomas M. Barnett)

# OTHER UNITS

The 7th Photo Group (Recon), which performed Photo and Mapping Operations, flew its first sortie in March 1943 and carried out 270 by year's end, losing 10 Lockheed F-4/F-5 aircraft. In 1944, 2,326 sorties were flown with 38 aircraft lost and 9 damaged beyond repair. In 1945, 758 recon sorties were flown with 5 planes lost and 6 damaged beyond repair. From January 1945, the Group used P-51D's to escort F-5s, and from March, P-51D and F-6 aircraft took over operations completely. During this period, to the end of hostilities, 853 effective escort sorties were flown with 5 Mustangs lost and 5 damaged beyond repair. Claims were 0-1-1. The 7th Group also operated some Spitfire IX's. Group markings on F-5s and Spit IX's were horizontal red bands on the cowling, sometimes with red spinners and/or rudders.

The 802nd Recon Group (Provisional), formed in April 1944, and the 25th Bomb Group (Recon), which was activated in England to absorb and replace the 802nd in August 1944, flew Weather and Reconnaissance Operations. In 1944, 1,897 effective sorties were flown with 9 planes lost (four in August) and 12 damaged beyond repair. In 1945, 1,484 effective sorties were flown with 8 planes lost and 2 damaged be-

yond repair. Twenty crewmen were KIA and 40 MIA. The 652nd BS operated B-24H and J and a few B-17G aircraft, the 653rd BS (Light) and the 654th BS (Special) operated De Havilland Mosquito XVI aircraft. Only the Mosquitos had unit markings — white aircraft letter on vertical fin within a white circle outline for the 653rd, plain white aircraft letter on vertical fin for the 654th, and the vertical tail or all tail surfaces red and spinners blue or red.

The 801st Bomb Group (Provisional) carried out Carpetbagger missions to supply the French Forces of the Interior and other patriot groups in Europe. It was formed with B-24s in December 1943 from the 4th and 22nd Antisubmarine Squadrons. Its first two squadrons were the 36th BS and the 406th BS. From May 1944 into August 1944 it also had the 788th BS of the 467th BG and the 850th BS of the 490th BG attached to it. Then in August 1944, the 801st took on the designation of the 492nd Bomb Group, the original such unit having been withdrawn from combat on 7 August, and its four squadrons subsequently had the designations of the original 492nd Group's squadrons — the 856th BS taking over from the 36th, the 857th from the 850th, the 858th from the 406th, and the 859th from the 788th. Later, December 1944, the 859th BS went to the 15th AF on detached service.

The mass of Carpetbagger Operations by the 801st/492nd, delivering food, arms, supplies, agents, leaflets, pigeon hampers and on one occasion a Jeep to the Continent or Norway at night, were conducted between January and September 1944. During that period, 3,511 tons were delivered. Peak month was July when 958 tons were delivered — 592 aircraft being dispatched and 437 making effective sorties to take in 100 personnel, 5,103 containers, 3,122 packages and 1,594 leaflets. In total, 25 aircraft were lost, 8 were damaged beyond repair, 197 crewmen were MIA and 11 were KIA.

The 801st/492nd operated mainly B-24 aircraft but also had some Douglas A-26s and some Mosquitos. Many B-24s and the A-26s had gloss black finish overall. Unit markings on B-24s were a yellow aircraft letter on the tail. The 406th BS, which went on to specialize on leaflet dropping, had the squadron code J6 and an aircraft letter in yellow on its B-24s which in general were black overall.

Leaflet Operations were first carried out (from 7 October 1943) by the 422nd BS of the 305th Bomb Group, then by the 406th BS from August 1944, and also by regular heavies participating in daylight operations. The latter dropped a total of 2,086.6 tons. In all, 237.3 tons of leaflets were dropped in 1943, 2,260.4 tons in 1944 and 1,236.7 tons in 1945 — a total of 1,493,760 leaflets. Three planes were lost, 5 damaged beyond repair, 16 crewmen KIA, 11 MIA, and 1 seriously and 10 slightly wounded. Claims were 3-0-1.

The 36th BS went on to specialize in Radio Counter Measure Operations in August 1944, with its B-24s taking over from and absorbing the 803rd Bomb Squadron (Provisional) which had operated B-17s in beginning such operations. The first RCM mission was carried out on the night of 5/6 June 1944. By year's end 608 aircraft had been dispatched with 574 flying effective sorties, and only one plane was lost and two damaged beyond repair. In 1945, 551 aircraft were dispatched with 536 making effective sorties at a cost of one plane lost and one damaged beyond repair. The 36th flew NMF B-24 aircraft with unit markings consisting of the squadron code R4 (which had also been used on B-17s of the 803rd) and an aircraft letter in black.

Air Sea Rescue Operations were at first carried out, from May 1944, by War Weary P-47D aircraft under the operational control of the 65th Fighter Wing. Then on 26 January 1945, the 5th Emergency Rescue Squadron was activated and took over operations, bringing Vickers OA-10A amphibians into use and, from March, some B-17G's equipped with lifeboats. In all, 3,616 sorties were flown of which 3,520 were effective, and two aircraft were lost, a P-47 in July 1944 and an OA-10A in March 1945. Unit markings on P-47s included the squadron code 5F and an aircraft letter, the cowl painted red, white and blue vertically, yellow bands around the vertical and horizontal tail surfaces and yellow wing tips. There were no unit markings on the all white OA-10A aircraft.

The 495th and 496th Fighter Training Groups received replacement pilots assigned to the Eighth Air Force and trained them in operational procedure, recognition of aircraft, ships and tanks, recognition signals, and gunnery. From December 1943, the 495th trained P-47 pilots and the 496th trained P-38 and P-51 pilots. Aircraft of these units bore the basic fighter unit markings of the Eighth, squadron code and aircraft letter. In the 495th, the 551st Fighter Squadron had the code DQ and the 552nd Fighter Squadron the code VM on their P-47s. In the 496th, the 554th Fighter Squadron had the code B9 on its P-38s, and the 555th Fighter Squadron had the code C7 on its P-51s.

Above left, P-47C, 41-6237, of the 495th Fighter Training Group; above right, Mosquito PR XVI, with H2X radar in nose for "Mickey" missions, of the 654th BS (Special), 25th Bomb Group (Recon); and right, Republic P-47D, 42-8496, 5F-X, of the Air Sea Rescue unit which later became the 5th Emergency Rescue Squadron. (Air Force Museum, Roy Ellis-Brown via Dana Bell, Ray E. Bowers)